THE SAVVY SHOPPER'S GUIDE

TO

THRIFT & CONSIGNMENT STORES:

GREATER SACRAMENTO, RENO/TAHOE

To Judy —
Happy shopping!
Jo Ann Philips

The Philips Group, Inc.
Reno, Nevada

The Philips Group, Inc.

P.O. Box 1507

Reno, Nevada 89505

www.joannaphilips.com

First printing, 2011

ISBN 978-0-9829268-2-6

Author photos by Stacy Hayden

Interior design by New Moon Graphics, Inc.

Disclaimer

The purpose of this book is to educate and entertain. The author and The Philips Group, Inc. shall have neither liability nor responsibility to any person or entity with respect to any loss or damage caused, or alleged to have been caused, directly or indirectly, by the information contained in this book.

DEDICATION

To shoppers everywhere who believe that paying full price is a sin. And to my mother, Gloria Gildone Philips, the Baroness of Bargain Shopping, who taught me everything I know.

ACKNOWLEDGEMENTS

I'd like to thank Lorraine McIntyre for her tireless and enthusiastic efforts on our shopping expeditions, and for her assistance in compiling the seemingly endless stream of information.

My graphic designer, Clif Edwards, helped me create the visual web that holds this book together.

CONTENTS

Acknowledgements 4

Introduction

Bargain Shopping: In The Beginning 9
Haute Stuff: The Appeal of the Deal 11
Bargain Shopping Defined 15
Second-Hand Chic: 19
Resale Rules for Buying 19
Consignment Cuisine: Rules for Consigning 23
End of the Line: 27
Rules for Donating 27
Savvy Shopping Secrets 29
Savvy Shopper Silhouettes 33

Consignment & Thrift Stores

Greater Sacramento
Antelope 37
Auburn 38
Cameron Park 43
Camino 45
Carmichael 47
Citrus Heights 51
Davis 58
El Dorado 64
Elk Grove 65
Fair Oaks 68
Folsom 71
Granite Bay 77
Grass Valley 78
Jackson 84

Lincoln...88
Orangevale...90
Penn Valley 91
Pine Grove...93
Placerville..94
Rancho Cordova 98
Rocklin 99
Roseville..102
Sacramento 112
Shingle Springs...152
Sutter Creek...153
Vacaville..154
West Sacramento 159

Lake Tahoe Area - California
South Lake Tahoe..160
Kings Beach..163
Truckee..164

Lake Tahoe Area - Nevada
Incline Village 169

Northern Nevada
Carson City...171
Fallon...177
Fernley...178
Gardnerville 180
Minden...182
Mound House 183
Reno...184
Sparks..200
Sun Valley 204

INTRODUCTION

I learned about the wisdom of bargain shopping at my mother's knee. When I was just a tiny tot, my mother, Gloria Gildone Philips, dragged me around the stores of San Francisco on Saturdays from early morning until late afternoon, just ahead of the commute traffic. We literally shopped until I dropped, shop-worn into her arms, fast asleep and clutching my bags of bargains.

My mother invented what I came to refer to as the "Shopping Olympics". I learned to leap tall rounders in a single bound, search for hidden treasures amongst the vast tundra of trash, grab the best merchandise away from women twice my height and ferret out fashion finds.

I learned how to tell the difference between real designer merchandise and knock-offs, quality merchandise and schlock, and adopted my mother's beliefs that everything is negotiable and that there is discount in volume.

My later training as a buyer for an upscale fashion chain store, showed me the wonderful world of wholesale, which, of course, further fed my bargain shopping mania. The idea that only people outside that world actually paid retail was constantly reinforced.

Years after my foray into fashion, I discovered consignment and thrift stores… and never looked back. To this day, the only thing that I buy new is food; everything else is gently used and formerly treasured. Even my license plate frames reflect my shopping passion: *Get outta my way, I'm going shopping!* and *This is not an SUV, it's a shopping cart.* My SUV is lovingly referred to as "the shopping shuttle" by my friends.

Speaking of my friends, it is at their urging that I write this book. They think that the treasure trove of thrift and consignment stores on my shopping route offers super shopportunities for bargainistas. So, here it is… happy shopping!

While we've combed the cities in this book to compile a complete list of thrift and clothing consignment stores, we realize that a few may have slipped through the cracks. If you don't see your favorite store on our list, please contact us at **www.joannaphilips.com.**

BARGAIN SHOPPING:
IN THE BEGINNING

"What a strong power there is in clothing."
Isaac Bashevis Singer

It's difficult to say when bargain shopping first began. The earliest shopping efforts were probably about trading: a buffalo skin for a winter's supply of food; a rifle for a mule; a homemade apple pie for a petticoat. It was about supply and demand. And when the supply exceeded the demand, the price went down: bargains were born.

The first recorded resale activity for clothing was in Paris in the early 18th Century. True to the Parisians' reputation for being fashion-forward, the "resale" clothing (in addition to fashionable fabrics, lace and jewelry) was actually stolen from the upper class and sold in the lower class underground for a fraction of the original cost (hence the term "getting a steal"). In fact, 28% of the criminal cases tried in Paris in 1710 involved stolen clothing.

The practice became very popular and was later legitimized via taxes collected on the hundreds of resellers doing business, according to tax rolls of the time. Since clothing revealed the "harmony of the inner and

9

outer man", clothes became the highly desirable "…weapons in the battle of appearance", according to The Culture of Clothing. Some things never change. You are what you wear; the mode of acquisition is immaterial.

THE DAWN OF THE DEAL

Resale clothing in this country has had its own evolution. The first resale store was reportedly opened by The Junior League, a charitable organization, in New York in 1914. They sold gently-worn clothing, accessories, toys, housewares, appliances and home furnishings. Other charitable thrift stores appeared by the mid 1930's, all designed to help the needy.

Today resale stores have broadened their focus in both merchandise and target customers, and are the fastest growing segment of retail business, totaling about 30,000 stores currently with sales reaching $12 billion, according to the National Association of Resale and Thrift Shops. Virtually recession-proof, the resale business has continued to increase at a steady rate of 7% for the past two years. According to industry reports, three-fourths of the stores surveyed reported an average 35% increase in sales for September-October 2010.

Once upon a time, there was a stigma about shopping at thrift and resale stores; however, in a recent e-Bay poll, 70% of shoppers say that it is socially acceptable to shop at resale stores versus five years ago. Almost one-third of American shoppers now buy pre-owned products, says WSL Strategies Retail, a consulting firm for the retail industry. In fact, 16%-18% of Americans shop at thrift stores yearly compared to 19.6% who shop at retail apparel stores, and 21.3% who shop a major department stores, according to National Association of Retail/Thrift Stores figures. Clearly, *thrifting* is now a fashion phenomenon.

As the resale stigma subsided, non-profit organizations expanded. Between 1999-2005, there was a whopping 67% increase in newly-registered 501C-3 charitable filings with the IRS (*Source: USA, 2006*).

HAUTE STUFF:
THE APPEAL OF THE DEAL

"I like my money right where I can see it - hanging in my closet."
~ Carrie Bradshaw, from *Sex in the City*

So, it seems shabby cheap has become shabby chic. The term *thrifting* is now a verb, not to mention a national pastime. Why the growing social acceptance? Let us count the ways:

• prices are a fraction of original retail prices and often 60%-

• 80% less on designer and better apparel, shoes and sporting goods

• you can still maintain an upscale lifestyle on a tight budget

• you can buy designer and better brands that you could not normally afford

• you can find items that are unusual, especially if you shop vintage

• you can be more trendy/stylish knowing that if your purchase

11

doesn't suit you, it can be resold or consigned, and because you didn't pay much for the item, your fashion faux pas is a free pass

- you can expand your wardrobe without expanding your budget

- you can turn over your wardrobe faster because the less you pay for an item, the easier it is to let it go

- you don't feel compelled to keep items forever just because they were expensive

- you can feel good about what you buy because you are paying less and have the ability to recycle what you buy (thereby recovering some of your initial investment)

- recycling your clothes allows you to shop guilt-free

- if you buy cheaply enough, you can re-consign at another store and make money

- in this down economy, resale shopping and consigning is a strategy for downsizing; you can't control the prices of gas or food, but you can control your clothing budget

- you can feel good about shopping at stores that fund charitable causes

- it's fun, like a treasure hunt

- it's an inexpensive outing with friends

- you feel like you are getting away with something when you find a bargain

What's not to love about this process? It's a win-win for everyone involved.

REMODELING THE FACE OF RESALE

Remember the old paradigm of a resale store - messy, disorganized, dirty, smelly, no fitting rooms, old items in poor condition, dimly lit? No wonder people rejected the concept, not to mention the presentation and merchandise. It was truly a discount disaster zone.

The chief complaint of thrift store shoppers in the past has been the offensive odor - rather like old socks, according to some people. Shopping is a sensorial experience, so when a shopper enters a store, it must *look* good *sound* good, *feel* good, and, of course, *smell* good.

Shoppers expect shopping venues to be pleasant, and since the majority of people are strongly visual, presentation is everything. Merchandise must be clean, in good condition, well-displayed by color, size and price. Lighting must be bright and cheerful. There must be fitting rooms with mirrors, relaxing music and friendly staff.

It's apparent that many of the thrift stores today have hired retail consultants to shape up their stores, and the results of the cosmetic surgery are dramatic. The stores have lifted, nipped and tucked their presentation and content putting a new face on thrift store shopping. Now they often compete with their retail cousins for the most beautiful shopping smile.

BARGAIN SHOPPING DEFINED

"A bargain is something you can't use at a price you can't resist."
~ Franklin P. Jones

We all know that bargains are goods and services acquired at less than their market value. The less the price, the better. So, here are the bargain store or off-price shopping options highlighted in our Guide:

CONSIGNMENT STORE

The actual term consignment, comes from the French word *consigner*, meaning "to hand over or transmit". Consigning, then is placing a person or thing in the hand of another, like clothing or furniture, but retaining ownership until the goods are sold.

A consignment store (consignor) takes new or used goods from a consignee (person consigning) and agrees to offer to sell the merchandise within a certain time frame to the public in a retail setting for a profit. *Used* may mean formerly-enjoyed, gently-used, prevouslytreasured, repurposed, redesigned and/or resurrected. The profit is usually split between the store owner and the consignee for anywhere from 40%-60%. Items are usually hand-picked by staff, kept for sale for 2-3 months, and then either donated, or retrieved by consignees. Consignees also have the option of purchasing items in the store with the credit accumulated in their accounts from the sale of their items.

Consignment is distinguished by:

1. The relation between the two parties is that of consignor (store owner) and consignee (person consigning)
2. The consignor is entitled to receive all the expenses in connection with consignment
3. The consignee is not responsible for damage to goods while in the possession of consignor
4. Goods are sold at the risk of consignor who also absorbs any profit or loss
5. Although consigned, title to the items is retained by the consignee

THRIFT STORE

Usually, a *non-profit* thrift store is one that accepts donated new or used goods which are then offered for sale in a retail setting to the public. The proceeds of those sales benefit a charitable cause or program.

The stores are usually owned by a charity or non-profit ministry but run as an independent business under contract; that is, the stores are licensed by the charity, which provides the goods for sale, and benefits by the sale of these goods directly to the contractor who operates the shop.

The store is staffed either by volunteers with a paid manager, or paid staff who may be involved in one or more of the charitable programs. Because the items for sale are donated, and there is no cost of goods, the items sold tend to be priced very low. Sometimes items are even offered free to qualified economically-challenged people with approved vouchers.

A *for-profit* thrift store generally buys its merchandise from charities in bulk to be sold for a profit to the public, again, in a retail setting, but the goods can also come from other sources like manufacturers and department stores with overstocked goods. Clearly a win-win situation, the charities that wholesale their goods to for-profit thrifts are able to further fund their programs from the proceeds, in addition to the goods sold at their own stores at retail.

Do you ever wonder what happens to all those donations that don't sell? Almost all non-profit thrifts stores sell their unsold textiles (unfashionable styles, stained or damaged fabric) to textile processors, who in turn, ship the processed goods mostly to Third World countries. In fact, almost half the garments donated to stores like The Salvation Army and Goodwill eventually end up in overseas markets as resale clothing or industrial fiber. (Source: "Old Clothes Go Global", *Seattle Times*, 2/25/07). Between 1999 and 2003, the U.S. exported nearly 7 billion pounds of used clothing and processed textiles. Talk about recycling!

Besides the low prices, the recycling of goods at thrift stores attracts many shoppers who like to "go green", considering themselves environmentally and globally-conscious. With the amount of jobs created through the recycling of donations nationally and abroad, you can understand the appeal.

RESALE STORE

A *resale* store is one that buys, sells or trades new or used merchandise and offers it for sale. If the store buys outright, they may offer the option to the seller of a higher price if they take a store credit versus a lower price if they take cash. These are very popular with young people in particular as a way to recycle their clothes while expanding and updating their wardrobes - for very little money.

17

A BARGAIN VS A DEAL

Bargain and *deal* are used interchangeably to describe merchandise that is offered at a favorable price for sale. It is also a perception because what is a bargain to one person may be only a slight blip on the mark-down screen to a seasoned bargainista.

The term *deal* indicates that there may have been some negotiating to arrive at a price low enough to be considered a deal, whereas a bargain seems to be a deal all by itself without the need to negotiate.

SECOND-HAND CHIC:
RESALE RULES FOR BUYING

"Buying something on sale is a very special feeling. The less I pay for it, the more it is worth to me." ~ Rita Rudner

As in any game, and let's face it, resale shopping is a contest to get the best items for the least amount of money, there are rules for buying. If you want to score in this secondary shopping market, here are some tips:

1. Visit a wide variety of stores and visit them often. New merchandise is displayed daily; if you snooze, you lose.

2. Pay attention to sale days. Many stores color code their merchandise and rotate their sales by color on a weekly or monthly basis.

3. Shop early, preferably in the morning when the store opens. The early bird gets the best selection.

19

4. Get in rapport with the store owners and managers. Let them know what kind of items you want. Develop a role as Owner's Pet.

5. Sign up for the store's mailing list, as they often have unadvertised specials.

6. Try on clothes whenever possible to avoid Buyer's Remorse. Sizing can vary widely and most stores have a no-return policy. And unless you are into retro, be aware of dated styles; look at skirt hemlines, pant flare and tie width. Not all resale stores carry fashion forward.

7. Pursuant to #6, examine clothing for quality. Remember your Home Ec sewing class and look carefully at fabric, garment structure, pattern matching, seams, buttons, buttonholes, fasteners and interior finishes. Any one of these criteria can be an indication of a quality garment, and as we know, quality transcends labels.

8. Check items carefully for damage. On clothing, look for missing buttons, tears, irregular sizing. On anything electrical or electronic, plug them in to make sure they work: appliances, hair dryers, TV's, lamps, computers, audio equipment.

9. Check cords for fraying or darkened areas which may indicate a previous fire. Most stores have electrical outlets you can use for testing.

10. If you like it, buy it! Carpe diem! It probably won't be there tomorrow.

11. Be patient. You may have to peruse quite a pool of prospective purchases to find your prize - that's why it's called *hunting* for bargains.

12. Shop resale online. Many stores offer convenient, user-friendly online catalogs. Ask about return and exchange policies for online catalog merchandise.

13. Ask about return and exchange policies at all stores.

14. Shop with seasons in mind. Shopping off-season can save you a lot of money. There are fewer shoppers clamoring for clogs in the winter or snow suits in the summer.

15. Develop a good eye and keen sense of value. It really helps to know quality. You could find Jimmy Choos in a sea of shoes.

16. Accordingly, know your retail prices of various labels, otherwise you have no basis of comparison.

17. Ask about coupons, senior discounts or specials that may not be advertised.

18. Watch your calendar. Many stores start marking down merchandise after 3.0 days, and if you can wait until just before a consignment contract expires or before the merchandise is donated, you can get a steal. Just ask the French.

19. Be aware of the store's sales policy. Some stores charge a buyer's fee on top of the purchase price. Be sure to ask.

20. Besides a cornucopia of clothing, resale stores often have killer deals on collectibles and used books. Leave no page unturned in your treasure quest.

JO ANNA PHILIPS

CONSIGNMENT CUISINE: RULES FOR CONSIGNING

"Anyone who lives within her means suffers from a lack of imagination."

~ Oscar Wilde

Each store has its own set of criteria for consigning goods. Most will give you a print-out of their specific policies. Here are some suggestions if you are considering being a consignee:

1. Make a list of the items you are consigning, to whom, on what date, and for how long. Many stores have their own consignment policies given to you to review and sign, but it helps to have your own inventory.

2. Before consigning, check out the store with the Better Business Bureau or an online credit bureau. Find out how long they have been in business, and ask about the payment policies for consignees. Read the online customer ratings to learn about any payment or policy issues.

23

3. Make sure that you understand the consignment policy. If you are unsure of anything, ask. Be sure to review the profit split, when and how you will be paid, and what happens if your items don't sell - can you pick them up and in what time frame? If your items are slated to be donated, at what price reduction and can you get a donation receipt? Ask about insurance liability for your items while they are in the store.

4. Be sure your items are in good condition, clean, pressed and on hangers. Ask for your hangers back once your items are accepted. Most stores prefer to use their own hangers anyway.

5. Check with the store to determine their definition of current style. Many stores won't take items more than two years old; however, classics like Chanel and Escada can be timeless.

6. Consignments follow the fashion seasons, so stay ahead of the curve and bring your items in accordingly: Spring items in March-April, Summer items in May-June, etc.

7. Keep track of your consigned inventory. Start a "Consign- ment" file. Many stores expect you to call or come in to see if your items have sold, and to get paid. Other stores will mail your check automatically or send you a notice that your items have sold.

8. Find out when you can consign items. Some stores require an appointment, some only take consignments on certain days.

9. Become familiar with the different kinds of merchandise in each consignment store so that you can match your consigned items to the store inventory. A junior store may not be interested in missy styles.

10. Along the same line as #9, knowing the price points and styles of various consignment stores enables you to shop for merchandise at one store and sell to another. Often, you can buy at a thrift store and consign the same item somewhere else.

11. If your items do not sell at one store, try another. Each has its own image and following.

12. Be sure to get a receipt if your items are being donated to a non-profit. Tax deductions are always attractive.

13. Donate rather than discard. If you are not inclined to consign, be sure to donate to a charity. Unless the item is totally shredded, it can help provide programs for the economically-challenged.

JO ANNA PHILIPS

END OF THE LINE:
RULES FOR DONATING

"Women love what they buy but hate two-thirds of what's in their closets."
~ Mignon McLaughlin

Most of us have more clothes than we will ever wear. In fact, it is estimated that the average woman only wears about 20% of her wardrobe. Some of the 80% that is not worn is due to weight loss or gain, undesirable gifts, and fashion faux pas that result in Buyer's Remorse. So, when you decide to downsize your clothing collection for what-ever reason, and you have exhausted your consignment opportunities for disposing of your gently-used and previously-enjoyed treasures, it's time to donate them to a worthy non-profit cause. Whatever your specific choice, use these as a guideline for dynamic donations:

1. Make sure that your items are in good, clean condition. They don't have to be working (depending on the item). In fact, learning to repair items is part of many job training programs that thrift stores support.

27

2. Call ahead to the organization to find out what items they will accept. Many don't take large appliances, and many don't pick-up donations.

3. Go through pockets, drawers, etc. to make sure that you don't leave any personal treasures in an item before you donate it.

4. Get a receipt for all donated items. Make a list of the items with corresponding values at the thrift stores while they are fresh in your mind. You may not remember how many skirts you donated in a month when asked by your accountant six months later.

SAVVY SHOPPING SECRETS

"A day without shopping is a day without sunshine."
~ Jo Anna Philips

Let's face it, shopping isn't really just shopping - it's what I consider *merchandise acquisition therapy*. I mean, who doesn't feel better after a day of scanning the sales, perusing before purchasing, and doing the deal - especially if it includes lunch with friends? The sight of shiny trinketries, the smell of exotic fragrances wafting through glittering beauty bars, the feel of cashmere between your fingers, the taste of raspberry lip gloss gliding across your mouth....it's truly a sensorial experience.

No matter what else is going on in your life, shopping brings joy - it is truly therapeutic, and it's usually much cheaper than the clinical kind. In the words of Tammy Faye Bakker, "I always say that shopping is cheaper than a psychiatrist."

So, if you are going to spend time enjoying this activity, it's good to know some Insider Tips gathered from years of experience. Even though we discussed the specifics for shopping at thrift and consignment stores, here are some all-around clever commandments:

29

1. Get the best price possible always. This should be your shopping mantra. It's also known as the *get-more-spend-less* theory of shopping.

2. Avoid trendiness and fads. Whether it's a jeweled bustier or skinny leopard jeans, *long term* means beyond lunch.

3. Avoid buying randomly or on impulse. "But it's cute", or "It makes me look younger" is not a strategy. Consider, "Does this go with anything else?", and "Will I really wear this?"

4. Frequent the malls for unadvertised specials and tune in to the media and internet for sales.

5. Cultivate friendships with the salespeople in your favorite stores. Good customers are rewarded, and bargains are built on relationships. In shopping at least, there are no laws against *insider trading*.

6. Be sure to sign up for every mailing list in every store in which you have a remote interest. This ensures not only mounds of mail/e-mail, but monetary rewards as well.

7. Arrive early to any sales. The early bird gets the best selection.

8. Avoid buying clothing for teens if they are not with you. Your idea of cool may not agree with theirs.

9. Likewise, avoid shopping with kids, in-laws or friends whose opinion of you conflicts with your self-image.

10. Along those lines, don't shop with anyone thinner than you, especially for clothing that shows more than 50% of your skin. Shopping with competitive friends can lead to a bigger diamond than you can afford or a shorter skirt than you can safely wear.

11. Shop for clothing in good light with lots of mirrors to reduce Buyer's Remorse. This is to make sure that the item fits you well, is of good quality and in good condition.

12. Don't be fooled by designer labels. Knock-offs are big business, so check a garment's quality: fabric, construction, buttons, seams, lining, fasteners. A garment's true value is in the workmanship, not in the label.

13. Run from anything lycra until either your body fat ratio has reached "0", or you look in a three-way rear view mirror first (see #11).

14. Avoid catalog shopping if you've had more than two alcoholic drinks. Likewise, don't buy big ticket items from studly types named Brandon (or women with cleavage named Lola). It's called *undue influence*.

15. Either write down or memorize where you parked your car, especially in large shopping centers.

16. Don't shop for groceries when you're hungry.

17. Unless you have a photographic mind, don't try to color-coordinate your wardrobe from memory.

18. Avoid buying clothing on vacation, remembering that an aloha shirt may not play well in Enid, Oklahoma.

19. Always check sizes on two-piece outfits and shoes to be sure that they match.

20. Make a mental note of your favorite items in the stores where you like to shop so that you know exactly where to go when you need something special.

21. Understand that the word "need" is not a word used in shopping. More appropriate are *love, cherish, adore, want, have to have* and *indicated.*

22. If you like it, buy it! When you see a sales opportunity, jump on it. If you wait, it may be gone with the wind.

SAVVY SHOPPER SILHOUETTES

So, we know that you are a bargain shopper, otherwise you would not be reading this book. But what kind of shopper are you? Over the years, I have categorized bargain shoppers into distinct personality types with shopping strategies to match. See which type fits you best.

VALUE VIGILANTE

This shopper has to buy at a discount. In fact, it is against her religion to pay full price for anything *ever*! She will negotiate the price of groceries, cars, medical and dental fees, movie tickets, insurance rates, child care, and of course, clothing, shoes and accessories. To her, shopping is a game - a contest to get the very best deal. She is absolutely driven; a woman on a mission.

This shopper embraces the *going-broke-saving-money* theory of shopping which says that as long as she is saving money, she can continue to shop beyond her limit. When questioned by any intrusive Significant Others, she replies, "But look at how much money I saved!"

33

SHOPPING OLYMPIAN

Like the Value Vigilante, this shopper is merciless when it comes to bargains, but she takes bargain shopping to a new physical level. She is able to leap tall t-stands in a single bound, carry massive amounts of merchandise to a check-out stand without a shopping cart, and while others shop 'til they drop, the Shopping Olympian is just warming up for more marathon shopping.

She can be an illusive character, dashing in and out of stores at lightning speed, shopping bags flying, her voice almost lost in the din. "I never met a mall I didn't like," she cries, smiling happily. She believes that anyone who says that money can't buy happiness doesn't know where to shop.

DESIGNER DIVA

This bargain shopper is a label lover, preoccupied with purchasing designer labels, at a discount, of course. She tends to frequent upscale fashion houses, consignment stores and super sales at department stores. She has a rigid set of fashion criteria, and wouldn't dream of wearing anything less. Somewhat elitist, she almost wishes she could wear her clothes inside out, labels flashing.

The Designer Diva is truly a clothing connoisseur who can identify designer styles with one eye open and even tell you what year they were popular. She can consume copious amounts of couture collection data, and can be a veritable treasure trove of information. Popular at fashion events, this shopper always wins bets as to which designer first used shoulder pads or which designer abhorred taffeta.

PERMANENT PERUSER

A Permanent Peruser is very picky. She loves to shop, but rarely buys anything. She simply loves the visual pleasure of scanning with her bargain antennae. When she does find something worthy of her attention, she experiences *paralysis by analysis*, and is incapable of making a decision. Too much information; too little time.

Also known as a *tire kicker* or *looky loo*, this shopper increases the frustration quotient of salespeople hoping for a purchase because no matter how vast the selection, she always finds something wrong. "It's not quite what I'm looking for," she genuinely laments.

HARRIED HOARDER

The Harried Hoarder knows that there is discount in volume, so she shops accordingly. Ever afraid of not having enough, this bargain shopper relies on her hunt-and-gather instincts to buy large quantities of sale items and stash them away - even if she already has a supply. She operates from fear (missed opportunity, limited quantity /price /color /size /style) and later from guilt and shame (exceeding her storage capacity at home, overspending, intruding on family living space). The fact that she already has seven blouses in the same color or more paper towels than blades of grass in her lawn does not occur to her until after her latest purchase.

This particular type of bargain shopper gives new meaning to the word *rummaging*, as she digs through piles of sale items du jour. She can often be seen peering over the top of her overflowing shopping cart, tottering with redundant purchases, muttering, "If one is good, ten are better!"

FLIPPING FASHIONISTA

Close to my own heart, this bargain shopper is a resale renegade - buying low at one store and reselling at a higher price somewhere else like another store or online. In real estate, it's known as *flipping*; in shopping, it's known as *savvy*.

Flipping is a short-term shopping strategy, so a Flipper buys an item with resale in mind, sometimes never even wearing her purchase. This kind of bargain shopping requires a vast knowledge of labels, market prices for those labels, and inventory of various resale and consignment stores. Sometimes the profit margin isn't great, but it's more the thrill of the deal.

NO-BOUNDARY BARGAINISTA

We all know one of these bargain shoppers - OCD and me makes three - Obsessive/Compulsive Darling. She has a passion for fashion and shops anytime, anywhere with anyone for anything. She lives, breathes, eats and dreams shopping. She doesn't wait for sales or other shopping events, and has been known to shop through rain, sleet and dark of night undeterred. She believes in shopping karma, and simply knows that she was born to shop.

She doesn't need an excuse to go shopping; in fact, the word *need* is never part of her shopping agenda. To this devoted dear, shopping is even better than sex, "At least if I'm not satisfied with what I bought I can exchange it for something that I really enjoy and not worry about hurting anyone's feelings."

Mention this book to your favorite thrift or consignment store and receive a discount on regular merchandise at participating shops!

CONSIGNMENT AND THRIFT STORES
CALIFORNIA: GREATER SACRAMENTO

ANTELOPE

GOODWILL
8031 Watt Avenue
Antelope, CA 95843
916-331-0237

Web Address: www.goodwillsacto.com

Hours: Monday - Saturday   10 - 8
             Sunday   11 - 6

Type of Store: Thrift, non-profit

Selection: Housewares and accessories, family clothing and shoes, electronics, toys, furniture, kitchenware, small appliances

Parking: Large strip mall

Easy Access: Highway 50 to Watt Avenue South

Prices:

Comments: Updated thrift store presentation - great for bargain hunters.

AUBURN

AMERICAN CANCER DISCOVERY SHOP
2376 Grass Valley Highway
Auburn, CA 95603
530-888-7434

Web Address: www.discoveryshop-auburn.org

Hours:
Monday - Friday	10 - 6
Saturday	10 - 5
Sunday	Closed

Type of Store: Thrift, non-profit

Selection: Collectibles, family clothing, shoes and accessories; housewares, furniture, small appliances, books.

Parking: Large strip mall

Easy Access: Highway 80 to Elm Avenue (Exit 119C)

Prices:

Comments: Unique quality resale experience.

AUBURN

CHIC BOUTIQUE
1269 Grass Valley Highway
Auburn, CA 95603
530-889-2442

Web Address: None

Hours: Tuesday - Saturday   10 - 5
                     Sunday - Monday   Closed

Type of Store: Consignment

Selection: Women's clothing sizes 0 - 16, shoes, accessories, jewelry

Parking: Parking lot

Easy Access: On Highway 49 at Canal Street

Prices:

Comments: Upscale presentation with lots of choices for the fashion-conscious.

AUBURN

COUTURE ANGEL CONSIGNMENT BOUTIQUE
111 Sacramento Street
Auburn, CA 95603
530-903-1097

<u>Web Address</u>: None

<u>Hours</u>:

Wednesday and Thursday	11:00 - 4:00
Friday	10:30 - 4:00
Saturday	10:30 - 5:00
Sunday	11:00 - 4:00
Closed Tuesdays	

<u>Type of Store</u>: Consignment

<u>Selection</u>: Women's clothing and accessories; small selection of very current styles

<u>Parking</u>: On-street

<u>Easy Access</u>: Off of Highway 80 East, Auburn Exit in Old Town Auburn in a mini mall

<u>Prices</u>:

<u>Comments</u>: Good things come in small packages. Tiny store, but great treasures.

 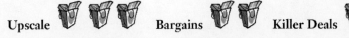

AUBURN

LOVED AGAIN CHILDREN'S BOUTIQUE
4076 Grass Valley Highway, #L
Auburn, CA 95602
530-887-5437

Web Address: www.lovedagain.net

Hours   Monday - Friday   10 - 5:30
            Saturday   10 - 5:00
            Sunday   12 - 4:00

Type of Store: Consignment

Selection: Children's clothing from newborns to size
12/14, accessories, shoes

Easy Access: Highway 49 past Dry Creek Road on right

Parking: Parking lot in Dry Creek Plaza

Prices:

Comments: Kids' shopping in an historic building.

Upscale   Bargains   Killer Deals

AUBURN

SALVATION ARMY
510 High Street
Auburn, CA 95603
530-823-3546

Web Address: www.salvationarmy.com

Hours: Monday-Saturday   9 - 7
               Sunday   Closed

Type of Store: Thrift, non-profit

Selection: Large selection in each category: clothing, furniture, accessories, electronics, housewares

Parking: Strip mall

Easy Access: Off Antelope Road in Citrus Heights

Prices:

Comments: Traditional thrift store presentation. Bargain hunters will love exploring the vast tundra of merchandise.

Upscale 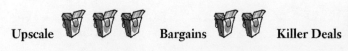 **Bargains**   **Killer Deals**

CAMERON PARK

SNOWLINE HOSPICE
2650 Cameron Park Drive, #240
Cameron Park, CA 95682
530-344-4480

Web Address: www.snowlinehoispice.com

Hours: Monday - Friday   10 - 6
                Saturday   10 - 4
                Sunday   10 - 3

Type of Store: Thrift, non-profit

Selection: Family clothing, accessories, shoes; electronics, housewares, small appliances, sporting goods, furniture, linens, books, toys

Parking: Strip center shared with Circle K

Easy Access: Highway 50 to Cameron Park Drive to Green Valley Road

Prices:

Comments: Newest of the Snowline Hospice stores

Upscale   Bargains   Killer Deals

CAMERON PARK

SNOWLINE HOSPICE
3300 Coach Lane, Building D-1
Cameron Park, CA 95682
530-676-8708

Web Address: www.snowlinehospice.org

Hours:
Monday-Friday	9 - 7
Saturday	9 - 4
Sunday	10 - 3

Type of Store: Thrift, non-profit

Selection: Lots of art and frames, craft books, tapes and CDs, knick knacks, furniture, accessories, limited clothing

Parking: Cameron Oaks Shopping Center

Easy Access: Highway 50 to Cameron Park Drive. Hard to find; look for western-style buildings in the rear of the parking lot.

Prices:

Comments: Overflowing with merchandise; lots of furniture displayed outside.

Upscale 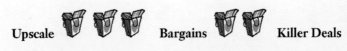 Bargains Killer Deals

CAMINO

SNOWLINE HOSPICE
3550 Carson Road
Camino, CA 95709
530-647-2703

Web Address: www.snowlinehospice.org

Hours: Monday - Saturday   10 - 5
             Sunday   11 - 4 (Sept. - Nov. only)
Type of Store: Thrift, non-profit

Selection: Lots of family clothing, shoes and accessories; even wedding dresses, books, kitchenware, art, toys, baby grand piano. Separate room for men's clothing

Parking: Dedicated lot

Easy Access: Off Highway 50 East at Camino, backtrack on Carson Road

Prices:

Comments: Rustic building is set in pine trees with beautiful view of the valley and mountains from the front porch. Stairs leading to the store are made of railroad ties which can be challenging to climb, especially with large items in tow.

Upscale   Bargains   Killer Deals

CAMINO

U-TURN FOR CHRIST THRIFT SHOP
5649 Pony Express Trail, #D
Camino, CA 95709
530-647-1004

Web Address: www.uturn4christcamino.com

Hours: Monday - Saturday   9 - 5
                Sunday   Closed

Type of Store: Thrift, non-profit

Selection: Family clothing, shoes and accessories; jewelry, housewares, electronics, small appliances, toys, books, sporting goods, furniture

Parking: Dedicated lot shared with U-Turn for Christ

Easy Access: Across from the Westhaven Hotel

Prices:

Comments: Very large traditional thrift store occupies two buildings.

 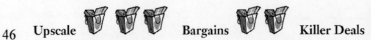

CARMICHAEL

GOODWILL
4126 Manzanita Avenue
Carmichael, CA 95608
916-481-6412

Web Address: www.goodwillsacro.org

Hours: Monday - Saturday   10 - 8
               Sunday   11 - 6

Type of Store: Thrift, non-profit

Selection: Family clothing, accessories and shoes; electronics, furniture, housewares, toys, books, small appliances, sporting goods

Parking: Strip mall

Easy Access: Off Fair Oaks Boulevard

Prices:

Comments: Traditional thrift store - great for bargain hunters.

CARMICHAEL

R THRIFT STORE
6634 Fair Oaks Boulevard
Carmichael, CA 95608
916-973-8081

Web Address: None

Hours: Monday - Saturday   9 - 8
              Sunday   9 - 5

Type of Store: Thrift, for profit

Selection: Family clothing and shoes, accessories, furniture, jewelry, housewares, eyewear

Parking: Dedicated lot

Easy Access: On Fair Oaks Boulevard near Manzanita

Prices: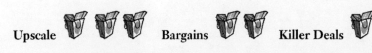

Comments: Consignment store presentation but thrift prices in an upgraded space formerly occupied by WEAVE. Barely-used furniture is on consignment. Daily discounts for Seniors.

Upscale   **Bargains**   **Killer Deals**

CARMICHAEL

THRIFT TOWN THRIFT STORE
6328 Fair Oaks Boulevard
Carmichael, CA 95608
916-480-0312

Web Address: www.thriftown.com

Hours: Monday-Friday   9 - 8
            Saturday   10 - 7
            Sunday   10 - 6

Type of Store: Thrift, for-profit

Selection: Large selection of family clothing and shoes;
accessories, housewares, toys, electronics, books, some furniture

Parking: Large strip mall shared by California Family Fitness

Easy Access: On Fair Oaks Boulevard

Prices:

Comments: Very large store with lots of shopping options;
updated thrift store presentation. Two more stores in
Sacramento.

CARMICHAEL

TICKLED PINK
7901 Fair Oaks Boulevard
Carmichael, CA 95608
916-971-1990

Web Address: None

Hours: Tuesday - Saturday   10:30 - 5:30
            Sunday   11:00 - 3:00

Type of Store: Consignment

Selection: Upscale women's clothing, shoes and accessories, formalwear and bridal

Parking: Small strip center

Easy Access: On Fair Oaks Boulevard before Manzanita

Prices:

Comments: Tiny space with select women's fashions in boutique setting.

CITRUS HEIGHTS

ECO THRIFT
7305 Greenback Lane
Citrus Heights, CA 95621
916-729-8474

Web Address: www.ecothrift.com

Hours: Monday-Saturday   9 - 7
               Sunday   9 - 5

Type of Store: Thrift, for profit

Selection: Largest for-profit thrift in the area; huge selection of clothing - men's, women's and children's; collectibles, handbags and accessories, jewelry, linens, housewares, small appliances, books, art, limited furniture

Parking: Large strip mall

Easy Access: Located next to Safeway at the corner of San Juan Avenue/Greenback Lane

Prices:

Comments: This is the thrift store of thrift stores. You can find major brands and designers at thrift prices; higher prices on jewelry and collectibles. Prices are color coded and sales colors change on Tuesdays.

Upscale Bargains Killer Deals

CITRUS HEIGHTS

FREESTYLE CLOTHING EXCHANGE
6412 Tupelo Drive
Citrus Heights, CA 95610
916-725-3733

Web Address: www.freestyleclothing.com

Hours: Monday-Saturday   11 - 7
                Sunday   11 - 6

Type of Store: Resale: buy, sell or trade

Selection: Women's and men's clothing, shoes and accessories;
some vintage

Parking: In front

Easy Access: Faces Highway 80 West at Antelope; hidden
behind the Salvation Army store

Prices:

Comments: Very youthful and fashion-forward with a junior
focus.

CITRUS HEIGHTS

GOODWILL
7120 Auburn Boulevard.
Citrus Heights, CA 95610
916-723-7382

Web Address: www.goodwillsacto.org

Hours: Monday - Saturday 10 - 8
        Sunday   11 - 6

Type of Store: Thrift, non-profit

Selection: Housewares and accessories, toys, electronics, sporting goods, family clothing and shoes, furniture, art, books, toys, small appliances

Parking: Strip mall

Easy Access: On Auburn Boulevard and Old Auburn Road

Prices:

Comments: Upgraded traditional thrift store - great for bargain hunters.

CITRUS HEIGHTS

MARY'S THRIFT STORE
7963 Auburn Boulevard, #2
Citrus Heights, CA 95610
916-729-0400

Web Address: www.marysthriftstore.com

Hours: Daily 9 - 8

Type of Store: Thrift, for-profit

Selection: Very large selection of family clothing especially for children; housewares, accessories, shoes, toys, jewelry

Parking: Large lot in Grand Oaks Center

Easy Access: Off Auburn Boulevard near Rusch Park

Prices:

Comments: Very traditional thrift store. Be prepared to dig for treasures.

CITRUS HEIGHTS

ONCE UPON A CHILD
7937 Greenback Lane
Citrus Heights, CA 95621
916-725-2525

Web Address: www.onceuponachild.com

Hours: Monday - Friday   9:30 - 7
            Saturday   9:30 - 6
            Sunday   10:00 - 5

Type of Store: Resale: buy and sell

Selection: Kids' clothing, shoes and accessories, furniture, toys, equipment

Parking: Large strip center shared by Marshall's

Easy Access: On corner of Greenback Lane and Sunrise Boulevard

Prices:

Comments: Everything for kids from newborns to sizes 16/18 youth. Also carry seasonal clothing like swimsuits and outerwear all year round.

Upscale Bargains Killer Deals

CITRUS HEIGHTS

SALVATION ARMY
6510 Antelope Road
Citrus Heights, CA 95610
916-729-8399

Web Address: www.salvationarmy/thriftstore.com

Hours: Monday-Saturday   9 - 7
                Sunday   Closed

Type of Store: Thrift, non-profit

Selection: Large selection in each category including clothing, furniture, pictures, housewares, small appliances, collectibles and jewelry

Parking: Strip mall

Easy Access: Off Highway 80 at Antelope Road

Prices: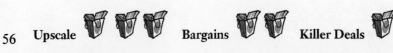

Comments: Very traditional thrift store. Bargain hunters will love exploring the vast tundra of merchandise; be prepared to dig.

Upscale   Bargains   Killer Deals

CITRUS HEIGHTS

THE THRIFT STORE #3
6150 Auburn Boulevard.
Citrus Heights, CA 95610
916-729-3173

Web Address: None

Hours: Monday- Friday   9 - 9
Saturday   11 - 6

Type of Store: Thrift, for-profit

Selection: Lots of seasonal clothes

Parking: Front, back and side

Easy Access: Auburn Boulevard at Greenback Lane

Prices:

Comments: Very low prices; traditional thrift store.

DAVIS

ALL THINGS RIGHT AND RELEVANT
1640 E. 8th Street
Davis, CA 95616
530-759-9648

Web Address: www.rrconsignments.org

Hours: Tuesday - Saturday   9 - 7
                Sunday, Monday   Closed

Type of Store: Consignment

Selection: Family clothing, shoes and accessories; housewares, books, toys, jewelry, art, See's candy, some vintage

Parking: Large strip center shared by Grocery Outlet and Dollar Tree

Easy Access: Short distance to Highway 80

Prices:

Comments: Updated thrift store presentation is affiliated with adjacent thrift store, R & R Thrift.

 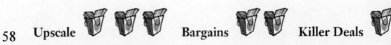

DAVIS

FRENCH CUFF CONSIGNMENT
130 G Street
Davis, CA 95616
530-756-3724

Web Address: www.frenchcuffBTQ.com

Hours: Daily 10 - 6

Type of Store: Consignment

Selection: Women's clothing, shoes, accessories and jewelry; some vintage

Parking: On street

Easy Access: Downtown Davis near the train station

Prices:

Comments: Perfect for nearby UC-Davis students seeking fashion at a price; piles of shoes. Very different from midtown Sacramento sister store.

DAVIS

HAUTE AGAIN
129 E Street
Davis, CA 95616
530-753-7008

Web Address: hauteagain@gmail.com

Hours: Tuesday - Saturday   10:30 - 5:30
         Sunday   12:00 - 3:00
         Monday   10:00 - 2:00

Type of Store: Consignment

Selection: Women's clothing, shoes, accessories and jewelry; some vintage

Parking: On street

Easy Access: Downtown Davis

Prices:

Comments: Can't miss the bright exterior colors in this tiny fashion nest. Loft upstairs houses vintage clothing, art and a cozy place to rest your tired shopping feet.

DAVIS

JUST KIDding
213 F Street
Davis, CA 95616
530-753-8687

Web Address: www.justkidsdavis.com

Hours: Monday- Saturday   10:30 - 5:30
                      Sunday   Closed

Type of Store: Resale: buy and sell

Selection: Clothing for newborns to size 10, toys, furniture and equipment

Parking: On street

Easy Access: In E Street Plaza at F Street

Prices:

Comments: Lots of choices and savings for tiny fashionistas.

DAVIS

R & R THRIFT
1640 E. 8th Street
Davis, CA 95616
530-759-9648

Web Address: www.rightandrelevant.com

Hours: Tuesday - Saturday   9 - 7
              Sunday   Closed

Type of Store: Thrift, non-profit

Selection: Family clothing and accessories, housewares, books

Parking: Large strip center shared by Grocery Outlet and Dollar Tree

Easy Access: Short distance from Highway 80

Prices:

Comments: Smaller version of adjacent sister store, All Things Right & Relevant. Traditional thrift store.

 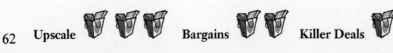

DAVIS

SPCA YOLO COUNTY THRIFT STORE
920 3rd Street
Davis, CA 95616
530-758-0544

Web Address: www.yolocountyspCAorg

Hours: Monday- Saturday   10 - 7
              Sunday   10 - 6

Type of Store: Thrift, non-profit

Selection: Family clothing, shoes and accessories; housewares, electronics, books, toys, sporting goods, small appliances, pet supplies, furniture, art

Parking: On street

Easy Access: Downtown Davis

Prices:

Comments: Festive flea market presentation, chaotic and fun; lots of furniture displayed outside.

Upscale   **Bargains**   **Killer Deals**

EL DORADO

ALL MY CHILDREN
6394 Pleasant Valley Road
El Dorado, CA 95623
530-622-1321

Web Address: www.shopatamc.com

Hours: Monday- Friday   10 - 6
            Saturday   10 - 5
            Sunday   Closed

Type of Store: Consignment

Selection: Infant and kids' clothing to size 14, shoes and accessories; books, toys, maternity clothing

Parking: Dedicated lot

Easy Access: Highway 50 to Ponderosa Road to Mother Lode

Prices:

Comments: You can't miss the charming yellow and white polka dot house. Other locations in Folsom and El Dorado.

ELK GROVE

AMERICAN CANCER SOCIETY DISCOVERY SHOP
8535 Elk Grove Boulevard
Elk Grove, CA 95624
916-685-7449

Web Address: www.cancer.org/discovery

Hours: Monday- Saturday   10 - 6
                     Sunday   10 - 5

Type of Store: Thrift, non-profit

Selection: Clothing, furniture, shoes, accessories, jewelry, housewares

Parking: Strip mall

Easy Access: Elk Grove Village off Highway 99 South

Prices:

Comments: Updated thrift store presentation.

<u>ELK GROVE</u>

<u>ONCE UPON A CHILD</u>
9163 East Stockton Boulevard, #370
Elk Grove, CA 95624
916-686-1666

<u>Web Address</u>: www.onceuponachild.com

<u>Hours</u>:

Monday- Friday	9 - 7
Saturday	10 - 6
Sunday	11 - 5

<u>Type of Store</u>: Resale: buy and sell

<u>Selection</u>: Kids' clothing, shoes and accessories; furniture, toys and equipment

<u>Parking</u>: Larger strip center

<u>Easy Access</u>: Near Bond Street

<u>Prices</u>:

<u>Comments</u>: Everything for kids from newborns to sizes 16/18 youth. A one-stop shop for your little ones.

ELK GROVE

THE CLOTHESLINE
8962 Elk Grove Boulevard
Elk Grove, CA 95624
916-714-4883

Web Address: www.theclotheslineex.com

Hours: Monday- Saturday   11 - 6
            Sunday   Closed

Type of Store: Resale: buy and sell

Selection: Women's casual clothing, accessories, shoes, jewelry

Parking: In lot and in back

Easy Access: In old Elk Grove on Elk Grove Boulevard at 33rd Avenue

Prices:

Comments: Boutique setting in historic library building.

FAIR OAKS

CINDERELLA COMPLEX
10149 Fair Oaks Boulevard
Fair Oaks, CA 95628
916-967-3552

Web Address: www.jaximage.com

Hours: Tuesday - Friday   10 - 5
                Saturday   11 - 4
                Sunday   Closed

Type of Store: Resale: buy and sell

Selection: Tiny store of vintage and current gently-used
womenswear and accessories

Parking: On street

Easy Access: On Fair Oaks Boulevard in Fair Oaks Village

Prices:

Comments: Cozy shopping in an intimate setting.

FAIR OAKS

MOTH HOLE
11787 Fair Oaks Boulevard
Fair Oaks, CA 95628
916-965-5542

Web Address: www.mothhole.com

Hours: Monday- Friday.   11 - 7
                Saturday   10 - 6
                Sunday   12 - 5

Type of Store: Consignment

Selection: Women's clothing, shoes and accessories; half the store has new goods, including designer samples, and the other half is consignment

Parking: Strip mall

Easy Access: At corner of Fair Oaks Boulevard and Madison in the Almond Orchard shopping center

Prices:

Comments: $5 racks outside. Very fashion-forward. Fabulous accessories with lots of bling. Mother-daughter owners make frequent trips to the fashion market for new styles and designer samples.

FAIR OAKS

PIXIE TRADERS
10144 Fair Oaks Boulevard
Fair Oaks, CA 95678
916-966-3249

Web Address: www.shoppt.com

Hours: Tuesday - Friday   10 - 5:30
              Saturday   10 - 5:00
              Sunday   11 - 4:00

Type of Store: Consignment

Selection: Kids clothing and accessories from newborns to size
10; maternity clothing

Parking: On street

Easy Access: In Fair Oaks Village next to the park

Prices:

Comments: Upscale fashions for mother and child. Additional
stores in Folsom and El Dorado.

 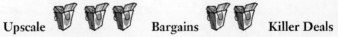

FOLSOM

BELLE MODE CONSIGNMENT BOUTIQUE
1012 E. Bidwell Street
Folsom, CA 95630
916-983-5330

Web Address: www.bellemodeboutique.com

Hours: Monday- Saturday   10 - 6
                Sunday   11 - 5

Type of Store: Consignment

Selection: Women's clothing, shoes, accessories, jewelry; some vintage

Parking: Large strip center

Easy Access: Off Highway, 50 East Bidwell exit

Prices:

Comments: Voted best vintage boutique by voters on KCRA 4 years in a row. Lots of labels; good selection of larger sizes.

FOLSOM

GOODWILL
390 Plaza Drive
Folsom, CA 95630
916-355-0364

Web Address: www.goodwillsacto.org

Hours: Monday- Saturday   10 - 8
            Sunday   11 - 6

Type of Store: Thrift, non-profit

Selection: Family clothing, shoes, accessories, jewelry,
furniture, electronics, toys, small appliances, housewares

Parking: Large strip center

Easy Access: Off Folsom Boulevard to Blue Ravine Road
Behind Winco

Prices:

Comments: Updated thrift store presentation - great for bargain
hunters.

 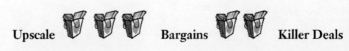

FOLSOM

KIDS TRADING POST
642 East Bidwell Street
Folsom, CA 95630
916-984-0714

Web Address: www.shopatktp.com

Hours: Tuesday - Thursday   10 - 6
             Friday - Saturday   10 - 3
             Sunday - Monday   Closed

Type of Store: Consignment

Selection: Kids' clothing, shoes and accessories from newborn
to girls' size 7 and boys' size 18; toys, books, some furniture

Parking: Strip center

Easy Access: On East Bidwell Street off Highway 50 at Blue
Ravine Road

Prices:

Comments: Charming shopping for the young and young-at- heart.
Additional locations in El Dorado and Fair Oaks.

FOLSOM

MARLA SUE'S CONSIGNMENT BOUTIQUE
1300 E. Bidwell Street, Suite 135
Folsom, CA 95630
916-984-6500

Web Address: www.marlasues.com

Hours: Monday- Saturday   10 - 6
            Sunday   Closed

Type of Store: Consignment

Selection: Women's clothing, shoes, accessories and jewelry

Parking: Large strip center

Easy Access: Off Highway 50, East Bidwell Street exit

Prices:

Comments: Caters to younger junior customers - small sizes.

FOLSOM

SNOWLINE HOSPICE THRIFT STORE
616 East Bidwell Street
Folsom, CA 95630
916-984-5853

Web Address: www.snowlinehospice.com

Hours: Monday- Friday   10 - 6
            Saturday & Sunday   10 - 5

Type of Store: Thrift, non-profit

Selection: Half family clothing, shoes and accessories and half furniture and housewares; jewelry, art, come collectibles, books, toys

Parking: Dedicated lot

Easy Access: Off Highway 50, East Bidwell Street exit

Prices:

Comments: Traditional thrift store; lots of good furniture.

FOLSOM

TRINITY THRIFT SHOP
412 Wool Street
Folsom, CA 95630
916-985-3870

Web Address: www.trinityfolsom.org

Hours: Tuesday   9 - 1
              Thursday, Friday, Saturday   10 - 1
              Sunday (2nd only)   9 - 1

Type of Store: Thrift, non-profit

Selection: Family clothing, shoes and accessories, linens, housewares, jewelry

Parking: In front and on street

Easy Access: Hidden off Sutter Street in old Folsom in old church building

Prices:

Comments: Located in a charming Victorian building, part of the church. Good selection for a small space.

GRANITE BAY

DESIGNER CONSIGNER
6945 Douglas Boulevard
Roseville, CA 95746
916-993- 3800

Web Address: www.designerconsignergb.com

Hours: Monday-Saturday   10:00 - 5:30
           Sunday   11:00 - 4:00

Type of Store: Consignment

Selection: Upscale women's clothing, shoes and accessories

Parking: Large strip center near Raley's

Easy Access: On corner of Douglas Boulevard and Auburn-Folsom Road in Country Gables Shopping Center

Prices:

Comments: Lots of labels: Dolce & Gabana, Ann Taylor, Nina Ricci. Tres chic. Mother and daughter owners. Mother started her original consignment store in London.

GRASS VALLEY

ANIMAL SAVE THRIFT & TREASURES
520 East Main Street
Grass Valley, CA. 95945
530-271-7071

Web Address: www.aimalsave.org

Hours: Monday -Friday   10 - 5
            Saturday   9 - 4
            Sunday   Closed

Type of Store: Thrift, non-profit

Selection: Family clothing, shoes and accessories; housewares, small appliances, sporting goods, linens, books and tapes, jewelry, pictures, pet supplies

Parking: Dedicated lot

Easy access: Highway 49 to Exit 182B Idaho/Maryland Road to East Main Street

Price:

Comments: Store sign says "Come in and adopt a cat or two". Fabulous felines are available for adoption upstairs.

 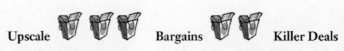

GRASS VALLEY

CANCER AID THRIFT SHOP
371 South Auburn Street
Grass Valley, CA. 95945
530-273-2365

Web Address: None

Hours: Monday- Saturday   10 - 4
              Sunday   Closed

Type of Store: Thrift, non-profit

Selection: Large selection of family clothing, shoes, accessories, jewelry, collectibles, housewares, linens, bridal

Parking: Limited on street

Easy Access: Highway 49 to South Auburn Street

Prices:

Comments: Oldest thrift store in the area. Charming adobe façade belies the large interior. Separate rooms for men's, kids. Brides-to-be will love the large selection of gowns. Adams family-like basement contains furniture and medical supplies.

GRASS VALLEY

ECO COMMUNITY THRIFT
122 Joerschke Drive
Grass Valley, CA. 94945
530-274-8983

Web address: www.ecocommunitythrift.com

Hours: Monday - Saturday   10 - 5
              Sunday, Monday   Closed

Type of Store: Thrift, for profit

Selection: Furniture, family clothing shoes and accessories;
linens, books, toys, pictures, jewelry, cd's/tapes/records

Parking: Dedicated lot

Easy Access: Highway 49 to Exit 183 to Brunswick Road to
Joerschke Drive

Price:

Comments: Updated thrift store with huge selection of old
records: 45's and LP's.

 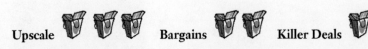

GRASS VALLEY

LIVING WELL THRIFT STORE
504 Whiting Street
Grass Valley, CA. 95945
530-272-9318

Web Address: www.livingwellgv.org

Hours: Monday -Saturday   10 - 5
               Sunday   Closed

Type of Store: Thrift, non-profit

Selection: Family clothing, accessories, shoes, jewelry, housewares, collectibles, books

Parking: In front and side lot

Easy Access: Highway 49 to West Empire Street to Whiting Street

Price:

Comments: The relaxing music in this boutique presentation makes for a great thrift store experience. Separate areas for men's and kids' clothing with collectibles in a special space.

GRASS VALLEY

MOUNT ST. MARY'S THRIFT STORE
410 South Church Street
Grass Valley, CA. 95945
530-265-1454

Web Address: www.mtstmarys.org

Hours: Tuesday - Saturday   10 - 4
                Sunday, Monday   Closed

Type of Store: Thrift, non-profit

Selection: Housewares, family clothing, shoes and
accessories; electronics, small appliances, sporting goods,
furniture, linens, books, toys, tools

Parking: Dedicated lot

Easy Access: Highway 49 to Exit 182A, left on South
Auburn Street to Neal

Price:

Comments: Located in historic St. Joseph's Cultural Center
next to Mount St. Mary's Academy. Fill your bag with
clothing for $5. on Friday and Saturday.

 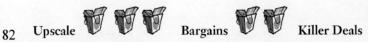

GRASS VALLEY

SALVATION ARMY
117 Neal Street
Grass Valley, CA 95945
530-477-1867

Web Address: www.salvationarmythriftstore.com

Hours: Monday- Saturday   9 - 7
              Sunday   Closed

Type of Store: Thrift, non-profit

Selection: Family clothing, housewares, furniture, small appliances, toys, books and some collectibles.

Parking: Dedicated lot

Easy Access: Off Highway 80 and Antelope Road

Prices:

Comments: Traditional thrift store.

Upscale   Bargains   Killer Deals 83

JACKSON

HEAVEN AND EARTH
126 Main Street
Jackson, CA 95642
209-223-1900

<u>Web Address</u>: None

<u>Hours</u>:

	Sunday, Monday	11 - 4
	Tuesday	Closed
	Wednesday - Saturday	11 - 5

<u>Type of Store</u>: Consignment

<u>Selection</u>: Women's clothing, shoes, accessories, jewelry, some men's clothing

<u>Parking</u>: On street

<u>Easy Access</u>: On Main Street in downtown Jackson, off Highway 49

<u>Prices</u>: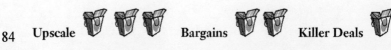

<u>Comments</u>: Boutique with lots of fab jewelry.

JACKSON

HOSPICE OF AMADOR THRIFT
10776 Argonaut Lane
Jackson, CA 95642
209-223-4762

Web Address: www.hospiceofamador.org

Hours: Monday- Friday   9:30 - 5:30
               Saturday   9:30 - 5:00
               Sunday   12:00 - 5:00

Type of Store: Thrift, non-profit

Selection: Family clothing and accessories, jewelry, furniture, books, housewares, toys, collectibles

Parking: Dedicated lot

Easy Access: Off Highway 49 in Jackson at Argonaut Lane

Prices:

Comments: Traditional thrift store.

Upscale   Bargains   Killer Deals   85

JACKSON

HOSPITAL AUXILIARY THRIFT STORE
539 South Highway 49
Jackson, CA 95642
209-223-5570

Web Address: None

Hours: Monday- Saturday   10 - 3:30
             Sunday   Closed

Type of Store: Thrift, non-profit

Selection: Family clothing, books, toys, housewares and accessories

Parking: Strip mall

Easy Access: On Highway 49 in Jackson close to the Waffle Shop

Prices:

Comments: Traditional thrift store.

 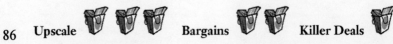

JACKSON

ON A MISSION
839 North Highway 49
Jackson, CA 95642
209-223-4250

Web Address: None

Hours: Monday- Saturday   9 - 5
           Sunday   Closed

Type of Store: Thrift, non-profit

Selection: Family clothing, shoes and accessories; jewelry, furniture, housewares, linens, art, kitchenware, books, toys, craft and sewing supplies

Parking: In front

Easy Access: On Highway 49 in Jackson

Prices:

Comments: Traditional thrift store with some fun collectibles.

 Upscale Bargains Killer Deals

LINCOLN

SALT CELLAR
454 "F" Street
Lincoln, CA 95648
916-645-1636

Web Address: www.thesaltminelincoln.com

Hours: Monday- Saturday   10 - 5
              Sunday   Closed

Type of Store: Thrift, non-profit

Selection: Collectible furniture, glassware, silver, art, books, and a section of vintage clothing

Parking: Along the adjacent street

Easy Access: Hwy 65 ends into Hwy 193 and one block to "F" Street

Prices:

Comments: Charming downtown Lincoln location, this is the collectibles store and retail presentation which is part of Vine Life Ministries' two-store chain; the other store is the Salt Mine.

LINCOLN

SALT MINE THRIFT SHOP
105 Floccini Circle
Lincoln, CA 95648
916-645-3503

Web Address: www.thesaltminelincoln.com

Hours: Monday- Saturday   10 - 5
                Sunday   Closed

Type of Store: Thrift, non-profit

Selection: Miscellaneous from soup to nuts: toys, books, family
clothing and shoes, furniture, lamps, golf clubs, children's
furniture, housewares, collectibles, wedding dresses, pictures

Parking: Ample parking with challenging configuration

Easy Access: Off Highway 65 North, access is somewhat
confusing; you have to make a sharp left off of 1st Street.

Prices:

Comments: A two-section warehouse and store. Excellent size
ranges, from petite to 3X and lots of shoes. Not your traditional
thrift store presentation.

Upscale   Bargains    Killer Deals   89

ORANGEVALE

BLOOMINGDEALS CONSIGNMENT
6231 Main Street
Orangevale, CA 95662
916-988-8662

Web Address: None

Hours: Tuesday - Saturday   10 - 5
           Sunday - Monday   Closed

Type of Store: Consignment

Selection: Small area of housewares and jewelry with some clothing and accessories; mostly vintage furniture and home furnishings

Parking: In front of store in small strip center

Easy Access: Off Greenback Lane

Prices:

Comments: Lots of treasures; embrace the hunt!

PENN VALLEY

HOSPICE GIFT & THRIFT
17440 Penn Valley Drive
Penn Valley, CA. 95946
530-432-7600

Web Address: www.hospiceofthefoothills.org

Hours: Monday - Friday   9:30 - 5:30
            Saturday   9:30 - 4:30
            Sunday   Closed

Type of Store: Thrift, non-profit

Selection: Housewares, kitchenware, family clothing, shoes, accessories, linens, jewelry, sporting goods, furniture, books, TV's

Parking: Dedicated lot in Penn Valley Shopping Center

Easy Access: Highway 49 to Empire Road to Penn Valley Drive

Prices:

Comments: Western-themed strip center has traditional thrift interior. Large selection of synchronized TV's.

PENN VALLEY

PENN VALLEY FIRE DEPARTMENT THRIFT
10513 Spencerville Road
Penn Valley, CA. 95946
530-432-2195

Web Address: www.pennvalleyfire.com

Hours: Tuesday - Saturday   11 - 4
                Sunday, Monday   Closed

Type of Store: Thrift, non-profit

Selection: Housewares, jewelry, accessories, family clothing, shoes, books, tapes/LP', furniture

Parking: Dedicated lot behind fire station

Easy Access: Highway 49 to Empire Road to Penn Valley Drive

Prices:

Comments: Hiding behind the Penn Valley Fire Station, if not for the small sign on the road, you wouldn't even know it's there. Appearances are deceiving, as this treasure trove is much larger inside than it looks. Lots of quality at garage sale prices! No charge for the laughs and goodwill of manager Maureen and her staff.

PINE GROVE

A THRIFT STORE
19728 Highway 88
Pine Grove, CA 95665
209-296-6999

Web Address: None

Hours: Tuesday - Saturday   11 - 6
                Sunday - Monday   Closed

Type of Store: Thrift, for-profit

Selection: Antiques and collectibles, art, tools, family clothing,
shoes and accessories

Parking: Lot next to Pine Grove Pizza

Easy Access: On scenic Highway 88 in the pines

Prices:

Comments: Everything and anything including a boat. You can't
miss the giant thrift store sign.

PLACERVILLE

NEW UNTO YOU BOUTIQUE
451 Main Street
Placerville, CA 95667
539-626-8700

Web Address: www.newuntoyouboutique.com

Hours: Tuesday - Sunday   10:30 - 5:30
              Monday   Closed

Type of Store: Consignment

Selection: Women's and juniors' clothing, shoes and accessories; eveningwear, jewelry

Parking: On street

Easy Access: Highway 50 to Main Street, Placerville

Prices:

Comments: A good place to go for dress-ups.

PLACERVILLE

SNOWLINE HOSPICE
3961 El Dorado Road
Placerville, CA 95667
530-622-1710

Web Address: www.snowlinehospice.org

Hours: Daily 9 - 6

Type of Store: Thrift, non-profit

Selection: Family clothing, furniture, housewares and accessories; collectible area, some appliances, tools, yard and garden, sporting goods, even player pianos

Parking: Dedicated parking lot

Easy Access: Highway 50 East to El Dorado Road

Prices:

Comments: Traditional thrift store.

   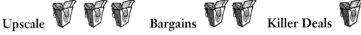

PLACERVILLE

SNOWLINE HOSPICE
455 Placerville Drive
Placerville Drive, CA 95667
530-621-1802

Web Address: www.snowlinehospice.org

Hours: Daily 10 - 8

Type of Store: Thrift, non-profit

Selection: Furniture and housewares: everything from player pianos to better glassware to lamps. Wide variety of general merchandise; smaller selection of clothing, wheel chairs/ walkers.

Parking: Dedicated lot

Easy Access: Off Highway 50

Prices:

Comments: Have to back track on Placerville Dr. Sits alongside a scenic creek.

 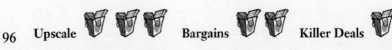

PLACERVILLE

VIOLETS ARE BLUE
450 Main Street
Placerville, CA 95667
530-626-8362

Web Address: None

Hours: Monday- Saturday   10:30 - 5:30
                Sunday   11:00 -4:00

Type of Store: Consignment

Selection: Women's clothing and accessories

Parking: On Main Street in downtown Placerville

Easy Access: Off of Highway 50 in downtown Placerville

Prices:

Comments: Organic sixties/seventies feel. Eclectic paintings on
the wall.

RANCHO CORDOVA

SALVATION ARMY
10309 Folsom Boulevard
Rancho Cordova, CA 95670
916-362-6296

Web Address: www.salvationarmy/thriftstore.com

Hours: Monday- Saturday   9 - 7
            Sunday   Closed

Type of Store: Thrift, non-profit

Selection: Family clothing, housewares, furniture, electronics, books, small appliances, art, toys and some collectibles

Parking: Dedicated lot

Easy Access: On Folsom Boulevard between Mather Field Road and Zinfandel Drive

Prices:

Comments: Traditional thrift store. Lots of furniture. Bargain hunters' paradise.

 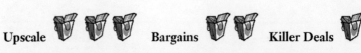

ROCKLIN

BON BON BOUTIQUE
6848 5-Star Boulevard
Rocklin, CA 95677
916-784-1697

Web Address: www.bonbonboutique.net

Hours: Tuesday - Saturday   10 - 5
                Sunday - Monday   Closed

Type of Store: Consignment

Selection: Women's clothing, shoes and accessories, jewelry

Parking: Large strip center

Easy Access: Off Highway 65 and Stanford Ranch Road across from Scandanavian Designs

Prices:

Comments: Lots of mid-range labels at moderate prices.

ROCKLIN

DOODLE BUGS CHILDREN'S BOUTIQUE
6827 Lonetree Boulevard
Rocklin, CA 95765
916-782-2215

Web Address: www.doodlebugschildrensboutique.com

Hours: Tuesday - Friday   10 - 6
              Saturday   10 - 5
              Sunday   12 - 5

Type of Store: Resale: buy and sell

Selection: Children's clothing and accessories from newborns to size 14/16

Parking: Strip mall

Easy Access: Lonetree Boulevard at Blue Oaks

Prices:

Comments: The store is almost as fun as the name.

ROCKLIN

UPTOWN CLOTHING COMPANY
5050 Rocklin Road
Rocklin, CA 95677
916-624-7474

Web Address: None

Hours: Monday- Friday   10:00 - 5:00
            Saturday   10:30 - 5:00
            Sunday   Closed

Type of Store: Consignment

Selection: Women's clothing, shoes, accessories, jewelry, prom dresses and eveningwear

Parking: In front

Easy Access: Across from Sierra College corner of Rocklin Road and Sierra College Parkway

Prices:

Comments: Boutique presentation of women's and junior fashions.

ROSEVILLE

AMERICAN CANCER SOCIETY DISCOVERY SHOP
1813 Douglas Boulevard, Suite B
Roseville, CA 95661
916-786-7773

Web Address: www.cancer.org/discovery

Hours:

Monday- Thursday	10 - 6
Friday	10 - 8
Saturday	10 - 5
Sunday	11 - 4

Type of Store: Thrift, non-profit

Selection: Small but select array of women's clothing, shoes and accessories; limited men's and children's clothing; furniture, home accessories

Parking: Large strip center shared by Ross

Easy Access: On Douglas Boulevard West near Highway 80, junction of Sunrise/Douglas

Prices:

Comments: Retail presentation with thrift store pricing.

Upscale 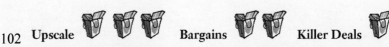 **Bargains** **Killer Deals**

ROSEVILLE

CHILDREN'S ORCHARD
1090 Pleasant Grove Boulevard
Roseville, CA 95678
916-787-5439

Web Address: www.childrensorchard.com

Hours: Monday- Wednesday   9 - 6
            Friday - Saturday   9 - 6
            Thursday   9 - 8
            Sunday   10 - 4

Type of Store: Resale: buy and sell

Selection: Children's clothing for newborns to size 12, shoes, accessories, toys, books, equipment, dancewear

Parking: Large lot in Highland Crossing Shopping Center

Easy Access: Highway 80 to Highway 65 to Pleasant Grove exit

Prices:

Comments: Bargain shopping for your little fashionistas. Ask about $5 fill-a-bag events.

ROSEVILLE

CROSSROADS TRADING COMPANY
1850 Douglas Boulevard
Roseville, CA 95661
916-781-9902

Web Address: www.crossroadstrading.com

Hours: Monday- Saturday   10 - 8
            Sunday   11 - 7

Type of Store: Resale: buy, sell, trade

Selection: Large and diverse inventory of young men's and
women's fashions, shoes, and accessories

Parking: Large strip center next to T.J. Maxx

Easy Access: On Douglas Boulevard off Highway 80 at Sunrise/
Douglas junction

Prices:

Comments: Great bargains on junior fashions.

ROSEVILLE

GOODWILL
1617 Douglas Boulevard
Roseville, CA 95661
916-783-0190

Web Address: www.goodwillsacto.org

Hours: Monday-Saturday   10 - 8
                Sunday   11 - 6

Type of Store: Thrift, non-profit

Selection: Electronics, family clothing, furniture, housewares and accessories, toys, small appliances, art, jewelry, shoes, small appliances, sporting goods

Parking: Large strip mall

Easy Access: On Douglas Boulevard West near Highway 80 at Sunrise/Douglas junction

Prices:

Comments: Updated traditional thrift store.

ROSEVILLE

GOODWILL
9400 Fair Way Drive
Roseville, CA 95678
916-355-0364

Web Address: www.goodwillsacto.org

Hours: Monday-Saturday   10 - 8
                Sunday   11 - 6

Type of Store: Thrift, non-profit

Selection: Family clothing, electronics, furniture, housewares
and accessories, toys, small appliances, jewelry, art, sporting
goods

Parking: Large strip mall

Easy Access: Off Highway 65 North - Pleasant Grove exit

Prices: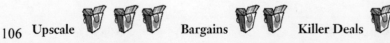

Comments: Updated traditional thrift store.

ROSEVILLE

ONCE UPON A CHILD
384 Roseville Square
Roseville, CA 95678
916-774-0852

Web Address: www.onceuponachild.com

Hours: Monday- Friday   9:30 - 7
                Saturday   9:30 - 6
                Sunday   9:30 - 5

Type of Store: Resale: buy and sell

Selection: Kids' clothing, shoes and accessories; furniture, toys and equipment

Parking: Large strip mall

Easy Access: One block off Highway 80 at Douglas Boulevard West

Prices:

Comments: Everything for kids from newborns to sizes 16/18 youth. A one-stop shop for your little ones.

ROSEVILLE

REVIEW BOUTIQUE
201 Walnut Street
Roseville, CA 95661
916-782-1877

Web Address: None

Hours: Monday- Saturday   10 - 5
              Sunday   Closed

Type of Store: Thrift, non-profit

Selection: Women's and children's clothing and accessories,
jewelry

Parking: Dedicated lot

Easy Access: End of Vernon Street in Old Town Roseville

Prices:

Comments: Located across from the train station on Atlantic, it's
a most charming 1940's house. Beautiful garden surrounds large
wrap around porch. Gorgeous hardwood floors throughout.

 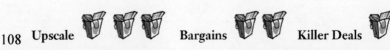

ROSEVILLE

ROSEVILLE HOSPICE THRIFT STORE
212 Harding Boulevard, #Q
Roseville, CA 95678
916-783-5509

Web Address: None

Hours: Monday- Saturday   10 - 6
            Sunday   11 - 4

Type of Store: Thrift, non-profit

Selection: Family clothing, furniture and accessories, jewelry, old records, housewares

Parking: Large strip center shared by Big Lots

Easy Access: Off Douglas Boulevard East close to Highway 80

Prices:

Comments: Carpeted and cozy, a smaller, more intimate thrift presentation.

Upscale 🛍️🛍️🛍️   Bargains 🛍️🛍️   Killer Deals 🛍️   109

ROSEVILLE

SPCA SECOND CHANCE THRIFT STORE
931 Washington Boulevard, #107
Roseville, CA 95678
916-782-2434

Web Address: www.placerspCAcom

Hours: Tuesday - Sunday   10 - 5
             Monday   Closed

Type of Store: Thrift, non-profit

Selection: Women's clothing, jewelry and accessories, some men's and children's; furniture and home accessories

Parking: Strip center

Easy Access: Off Douglas Boulevard East in Roseville Business Park

Prices:

Comments: Newest SPCA effort is the new face of thrift retail: an upscale boutique with thrift pricing. Killer deals on very gently- used current styles.

 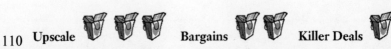

ROSEVILLE

ST. VINCENT DE PAUL
1000 Melody Lane, #109
Roseville, CA   95825
916-781-3303

Web Address: www.svdp-sacramento.org

Hours: Monday- Saturday   10 - 8
               Sunday   12 - 5

Type of Store: Thrift, non-profit

Selection: housewares, furniture, family clothing, toys, books, collectibles, toys

Parking: Large strip mall

Easy Access: Off Highway 80 to Cirby to Melody Lane

Prices:

Comments: Very traditional thrift store.

Upscale 🛍️🛍️🛍️ **Bargains** 🛍️🛍️ **Killer Deals** 🛍️

SACRAMENTO

AMERICAN CANCER SOCIETY DISCOVERY SHOP
2744 Marconi Drive
Sacramento, CA 95821
916-484-0227

Web Address: www.discoveryshop-sacramento.org

Hours: Monday- Friday   10 - 6
             Saturday   10 - 5
             Sunday   12 - 5

Type of Store: Thrift, non-profit

Selection: Large selection of furniture, women's (some men's) clothing and accessories, jewelry, housewares

Parking: Large lot in Taylor Center

Easy Access: Corner of Marconi and Fulton

Prices:

Comments: Exceptional retail presentation with large selection of barely-used furniture and home accessories.

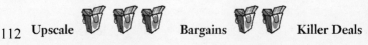

Upscale   **Bargains**   **Killer Deals**

SACRAMENTO

ARTICLE CONSIGNMENT BOUTIQUE
5704 Elvas Avenue
Sacramento, CA 95819
916-316-5772

Web Address: www.articleconsignment.com

Hours: Tuesday, Wednesday, Saturday   10:30 - 6
        Thursday - Friday   10:30 - 7
        Sunday - Monday   Closed

Type of Store: Consignment

Selection: Women's and men's clothing shoes and accessories;
jewelry, handmade soap, accessories and gift cards from local
artisans

Parking: On street and shared lot

Easy Access: Highway 50 to 65th Street to Elvas Street

Prices:

Comments: Winner of Sacramento Magazine's Best Place to
Party in Style, the venue is available for small events. Lots
of labels in a charming boutique setting.

Upscale   Bargains   Killer Deals   113

SACRAMENTO

ASSISTANCE LEAGUE THRIFT SHOP
2528 Yorktown Avenue, #C
Sacramento, CA 95821
916-488-0828

Web Address: www.assistanceleague.org

Hours: Monday- Saturday   10 - 4
               Sunday   Closed

Type of Store: Thrift, non-profit

Selection: Clothing for women and men, housewares, accessories, buttons, books, leather coats, shoes

Parking: In front of store

Easy Access: Off Watt Avenue and El Camino

Prices:

Comments: Traditional thrift store.

Bargains   Killer Deals

SACRAMENTO

BABIES AND BEYOND
2996 Freeport Boulevard
Sacramento, CA 95818
916-441-5200

Web Address: www.babiesandbeyondstore.com

Hours: Tuesday - Thursday   11 - 5:30
                Friday   11 - 6:00
                Saturday   11 - 5:00
                Sunday   11 - 4:00

Type of Store: Resale: buy and sell

Selection: Clothing for infants through children's size 8/10, shoes, accessories, furniture, books, toys; maternity clothes through size 3.X

Parking: On street or in adjacent small lot

Easy Access: Off Capitol Freeway at Freeport Boulevard

Prices:

Comments: Fun shopping for moms and moms-to-be.

Upscale Bargains Killer Deals

SACRAMENTO

BOWS AND ARROWS
1815 19th Street
Sacramento, CA 95816
916-822-5668

Web Address: http://www.etsy.com/shop/bowsandarrowsvintage

Hours: Daily 11 - 11

Type of Store: Resale - buy, sell, trade

Selection: Large selection of vintage clothing and accessories for women, jewelry, some menswear

Parking: On street

Easy Access: Off Highway 50 East, 16th Street exit

Prices: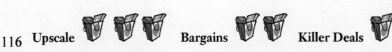

Comments: Located in mid-town Sacramento, this store is fun, young and hip - in a retro way. Clothing is arranged by decade from 1950s to 1980s. New addition of café, art gallery and performance area.

SACRAMENTO

CRIMSON AND CLOVER
1617 16th Street
Sacramento, CA 95814
916-442-1800

Web Address: www.crimsonandcloverboutique.com

Hours: Tuesday - Thursday, Saturday   11 - 7
               Friday   12 - 8
               Sunday   Closed

Type of Store: Resale

Selection: Women's truly vintage clothing, shoes, accessories, lingerie

Parking: On street

Easy Access: Midtown on 16th Street between P & Q Streets across from Fremont Park

Prices:

Comments: Charming and romantic boutique full of affordable treasures from bygone eras.

SACRAMENTO

CROSSROADS TRADING COMPANY
2935 Arden Way
Sacramento, CA 95825
916-972-9900

Web Address: ww.crossroadstrading.com

Hours: Monday- Saturday   10 - 8
              Sunday   11 - 7

Type of Store: Resale: buy, sell, trade

Selection: Large collection of young women's and men's fashions, shoes and accessories

Parking: Large strip mall

Easy Access: On Arden Way between Morse and Fulton

Prices:

Comments: Great bargains for junior fashionistas.

SACRAMENTO

DESERET INDUSTRIES
3000 Auburn Boulevard, #B
Sacramento, CA 95821
916-482-1480

Web Address: None

Hours:

	Monday	9 - 6
	Tuesday - Friday	9 - 8
	Saturday	9 - 7
	Sunday	Closed

Type of Store: Thrift, non-profit

Selection: Huge store with a large selection in every category: clothing, furniture, housewares and accessories, shoes, electronics, toys, kitchenware

Parking: Dedicated lot

Easy Access: Off Auburn Boulevard at Winding Way near Highway 80

Prices:

Comments: Very large traditional thrift store. Be sure to check out the back room for furniture and accessory bargains.

Upscale   Bargains   Killer Deals   119

SACRAMENTO

ECO THRIFT
4220 Fruitridge Road
Sacramento, CA 95820
916-391-2402

Web Address: www.ecothrift.com

Hours: Monday- Saturday   9 - 7
                Sunday   10 - 6

Type of Store: Thrift, for profit

Selection: Largest for-profit in the area; huge collection of all
categories: family clothing, shoes, accessories, jewelry, handbags,
housewares, bed linens, collectibles, art, small appliances, electronics

Parking: Dedicated lot

Easy Access: Off Highway 99 South

Prices:

Comments: Along with its sister location in Citrus Heights, this is the
thrift store of thrift stores. Designer labels and well-known brands at
killer prices. Prices are color-coded and sales colors change on
Tuesdays.

SACRAMENTO

ED'S THREADS
1125 21st Street
Sacramento, CA 95811
916-446-8138

Web Address: None

Hours: Tuesday, Wednesday, Friday - Sunday   10 - 5
             Monday, Thursday   Closed

Type of Store: Resale: buy and sell

Selection: Men's vintage clothing, shoes and accessories

Parking: On street

Easy Access: Midtown 21st Street at L Street

Prices:

Comments: Finally, something for the guys - cool fashions from the 1940's - 1960's. Located in an historical brick building; in business for 30 years.

Upscale   Bargains   Killer Deals   121

SACRAMENTO

EMMANUEL THRIFT STORE
4120 El Camino
Sacramento, CA 95864
916-285-5476

Web Address: None

Hours: Monday- Saturday   10 - 6
              Sunday   11 - 4

Type of Store: Thrift, for profit

Selection: Family clothing, shoes and accessories; electronics, housewares, small appliances, sporting goods, furniture, linens, books, toys, tools

Parking: Ample lot in Del Paso Manor

Easy Access: Eastern Avenue to El Camino

Prices:

Comments: Very traditional thrift store presentation. A table for local entrepreneurs contains books, crafts, gift cards, handmade items for sale on consignment.

SACRAMENTO

FAMILY TREE THRIFT SHOPPE
9181 Kiefer Boulevard
Sacramento, CA 95826
918-361-7445

Web Address: None

Hours: Monday- Saturday   9 - 7
            Sunday   10 - 6

Type of Store: Thrift, non-profit

Selection: Family clothing, toys, housewares, furniture, electronics, games, books, CD's

Parking: Large strip center next to UPS

Easy Access: Off Highway 50 at Watt Avenue South

Prices:

Comments: Traditional thrift store.

Upscale  Bargains Killer Deals

SACRAMENTO

FREESTYLE CLOTHING EXCHANGE
2101 L Street
Sacramento, CA 95816
916-441-3733

Web Address: www.freestyleclothing.com

Hours: Monday- Saturday   11 - 7
                Sunday   11 - 6

Type of Store: Resale: buy, sell, trade

Selection: Women's and men's clothing, shoes and accessories

Parking: On street

Easy Access: In mid-town at 21st Street

Prices:

Comments: Very fashion-forward with a junior focus.

SACRAMENTO

FRENCH CUFF CONSIGNMENT
2527 J Street
Sacramento, CA 95816
916-442-3724

Web Address: www.frenchcuffbtq.com

Hours: Daily 10 - 6

Type of Store: Consignment

Selection: Upscale women's clothing, shoes and accessories including eveningwear

Parking: On street

Easy Access: Heart of Mid-town Sacramento between 25th and 26th Streets

Prices:

Comments: Labels, labels, labels - you name it, they've got it. Sophisticated presentation in boutique setting. Lots of bling for fashionistas. Second store in Davis.

Upscale Bargains Killer Deals   125

SACRAMENTO

FRINGE
2409 21st Street
Sacramento, CA 95818
916-706-0216

Web Address: www.fringeofpelika.com

Hours: Monday, Tuesday   Closed
            Wednesday- Saturday   11 - 6
            Sunday   11 - 4

Type of Store: Resale vintage with some consignment

Selection: From cowboy boots to hats, jewelry, accessories, handbags

Parking: On street

Easy Access: Mid-town Sacramento

Prices:

Comments: Lots of kitsch and mid-town hip, an eclectic fantasy.

SACRAMENTO

GOODWILL
4040 Florin Road
Sacramento, CA 95630
916-355-0364

Web Address: www.goodwillsacto.com

Hours: Monday- Saturday   10 - 8
            Sunday   11 - 6

Type of Store: Thrift, non-profit

Selection: Family clothing, shoes, accessories, jewelry, furniture
electronics, toys, small appliances, housewares, books, art, sporting
goods

Parking: Strip center

Easy Access: Off "I" Street to Florin

Prices:

Comments: Traditional thrift store; great for bargain hunters.

Upscale   Bargains   Killer Deals

SACRAMENTO

GOODWILL
6648 Franklin Boulevard
Sacramento, CA 95823
916-395-9023

Web Address: www.goodwillsacto.com

Hours: Monday- Saturday   9 - 8
              Sunday   11 - 6

Type of Store: Thrift, non-profit

Selection: Family clothing, shoes and accessories; furniture,
housewares, books, jewelry, toys, small appliances, sporting goods,
electronics

Parking: Multi-use center

Easy Access: Corner of Franklin Boulevard and Martin Luther
King, Jr. in Southgate Industrial Park

Prices:

Comments: Traditional thrift store; great for bargain hunters.

 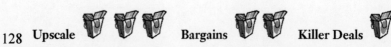

SACRAMENTO

GOODWILL
1312 Fulton Avenue
Sacramento, CA 95825
916-979-1651

Web Address: www.goodwillsacto.com

Hours: Monday- Saturday   10 - 8
                Sunday   11 - 6

Type of Store: Thrift, non-profit

Selection: Family clothing, shoes, accessories, jewelry, furniture, electronics, toys, small appliances, housewares

Parking: Strip center

Easy Access: Fair Oaks to Munroe to Fulton

Prices:

Comments: Traditional thrift store - great for bargain hunters.

Upscale   Bargains   Killer Deals

SACRAMENTO

GOODWILL
5705 Hillsdale Boulevard
Sacramento, CA 95842
916-339-2137

Web Address: www.goodwillsacto.com

Hours: Monday- Saturday   10 - 8
               Sunday   11 - 6

Type of Store: Thrift, non-profit

Selection: Family clothing, shoes, accessories, jewelry, furniture, electronics, toys, small appliances, housewares, books, sporting goods

Parking: Large lot

Easy Access: Walerga Boulevard to Hillsdale Boulevard

Prices:

Comments: Traditional thrift store - great for bargain hunters.

SACRAMENTO

GOODWILL
1621 "L" Street
Sacramento, CA 95814
916-441-4407

Web Address: www.goodwillsacto.com

Hours: Monday - Saturday   10 - 6
              Sunday   11 - 6

Type of Store: Thrift, non-profit

Selection: Family clothing, shoes and accessories; housewares, linens, small appliances, books/cd's/tapes

Parking: On street

Easy Access: 16th Street to "L" Street

Prices:

Comments: Goodwill's latest foray into upscale boutique presentation in mid-town; used brick walls, polished wood floors. Lots of XL sizes and entire wall of handbags.

SACRAMENTO

GOODWILL
7207 Norwood Avenue
Sacramento, CA 95838
916-649-2531

Web Address: www.goodwillsacto.com

Hours: Monday- Saturday   10 - 9
              Sunday   11 - 6

Type of Store: Thrift, non-profit

Selection: Family clothing, shoes, accessories, jewelry, furniture, electronics, toys, small appliances, housewares, sporting goods

Parking: Strip mall

Easy Access: Norwood exit off I-80

Prices:

Comments: Traditional thrift store - great for bargain hunters.

 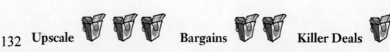

SACRAMENTO

GOODWILL
2502 Watt Avenue
Sacramento, CA 95821
916-480-9002

Web Address: www.goodwillsacto.com

Hours: Monday- Saturday   10 - 8
               Sunday   11 - 6

Type of Store: Thrift, non-profit

Selection: Family clothing, shoes, accessories, jewelry, furniture, electronics, toys, small appliances, housewares, books

Parking: Large strip mall

Easy Access: Off Highway 50 at Watt Avenue South

Prices:

Comments: Updated thrift store presentation - great for bargain hunters.

SACRAMENTO

HEFTY NIFTY THRIFTY STORE
4620 Watt Avenue
Sacramento, CA 95660
916-485-5510

Web Address: None

Hours: Monday- Saturday   9:30 - 6
                Sunday   Closed

Type of Store: Consignment

Selection: Clothing, shoes, accessories, housewares

Parking: Shared lot

Easy Access: Off Highway 80 at Watt

Prices: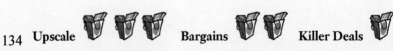

Comments: Consignment with thrift store presentation.

SACRAMENTO

LULU FOREVER
315 33rd Street
Sacramento, CA 95816
916-444-7309

Web Address: None

Hours: Monday- Saturday   10 - 6
            Sunday   Closed

Type of Store: Resale: buy and sell

Selection: Women's vintage clothing, shoes and accessories; some menswear

Parking: On street and in lot next door

Easy Access: Off McKinley Boulevard near McKinley Park

Prices:

Comments: For Retro Rats and beyond.

SACRAMENTO

ONCE UPON A CHILD
3186 Arden Way
Sacramento, CA 95825
916-488-8861

Web Address: www.onceuponachild.com

Hours: Monday- Friday   9:30 - 7:30
            Saturday   10:00 - 6:00
            Sunday   11:00 - 5:00

Type of Store: Resale: buy and sell

Selection: Kids' clothing, shoes and accessories; furniture, toys and equipment

Parking: Large shared lot

Easy Access: On Arden Way between Morse and Watt Avenues

Prices:

Comments: Everything for kids from newborns to sizes 16/18 youth. A one-stop shop for your little ones.

SACRAMENTO

RENAISSANCE FINE CONSIGNMENT
2362 Fair Oaks Boulevard
Sacramento, CA 95826
916-485-4911

Web Address: www.renaissancecorp.com

Hours: Monday, Tuesday   10:00 - 6:30
          Wednesday - Friday   10:00 - 8:00
          Sunday   11:00 - 5:00

Type of Store: Consignment

Selection: Women's upscale clothing, shoes, accessories, jewelry, and vintage

Parking: Strip center

Easy Access: On Fair Oak Boulevard across from Loehmann's Plaza

Prices:

Comments: Great shopping for the well-dressed conservative who is label-conscious. Large selection of eveningwear.

Upscale   Bargains   Killer Deals   137

SACRAMENTO

SALVATION ARMY
315 16th Street
Sacramento, CA 95816
916-448-0890

Web Address: www.salvationarmy/thriftstore.com

Hours: Monday-Saturday   9 - 7
                 Sunday   Closed

Type of Store: Thrift, non-profit

Selection: Large in each category - clothing, furniture, accessories, shoes, collectibles, electronics, housewares, small appliances, books, toys

Parking: Dedicated lot

Easy Access: Highway 50 to 16th & D Streets

Prices:

Comments: Very traditional thrift store.

SACRAMENTO

SEQUELS CONSIGNMENT BOUTIQUE
523 Munroe Street
Sacramento, CA 95826
916-489-1545

Web Address: www.consignmentatsequels.com

Hours: Monday- Friday   11 - 6
        Saturday   11 - 5
        Sunday, Monday   Closed

Type of Store: Consignment

Selection: Upscale select women's clothing, shoes, jewelry and accessories; lots of petite and small sizes

Parking: Large lot in Loehmann's Plaza

Easy Access: Off Fair Oaks Boulevard on the east side of Loehmann's Plaza facing Munroe

Prices:

Comments: Owner is an interior designer, which is reflected in her charming boutique. Mascot Barkley acts as her canine concierge. Super shopportunities for slender trendenistas.

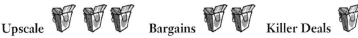
Upscale   Bargains   Killer Deals   139

SACRAMENTO

SPCA WOMEN'S Guild Thrift
1517 E Street
Sacramento, CA 95814
916-442-8118

Web Address: www.aspca.org

Hours: Tuesday - Friday   10 - 6
Saturday   10 - 5
Sunday   12 - 5

Type of Store: Thrift, non-profit

Selection: Large selection of men's and women's clothing, shoes and accessories; jewelry, housewares, art, kitchenware, furniture, vintage clothing

Parking: Small side lot and on street

Easy Access: Mid-town at 16th and E Streets

Prices: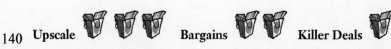

Comments: Traditional thrift store; separate room for vintage clothing.

SACRAMENTO

ST. PATRICK'S THRIFT STORE
5960 Franklin Boulevard
Sacramento, CA 95824
916-422-8391

Web Address: None

Hours: Monday- Saturday   10 - 4
                Sunday   Closed

Type of Store: Thrift, non-profit

Selection: Family clothing, furniture, books, shoes, home accessories

Parking: Shared lot

Easy Access: Highway 99 South to Fruitridge Road

Prices:

Comments: Traditional thrift store located across from St. Rose Church.

SACRAMENTO

ST. VINCENT DE PAUL THRIFT STORE
2275 Watt Avenue
Sacramento, CA 95825
916-972-1212

Web Address: None

Hours: Monday- Saturday   10 - 8
            Sunday   12 - 5

Type of Store: Thrift, non-profit

Selection: Large selection of family clothing, furniture, home
accessories, collectibles, books, glassware

Parking: Dedicated lot

Easy Access: Highway 50 to North Watt Avenue

Prices:

Comments: Traditional thrift store with charming separate rooms for
collectible metal ware (copper, brass, silver), books, vintage clothing,
videos/CDs and glassware.

SACRAMENTO

TEEN CHALLENGE THRIFT STORE
10025 Folsom Boulevard
Sacramento, CA 95827
916-369-5422

Web Address: www.sacramentovalleythrift@teenchallenge.com

Hours: Monday- Friday   9 - 8
            Saturday   10 - 5
            Sunday   Closed

Type of Store: Thrift, non-profit

Selection: Family clothing, linens, electronics, furniture, housewares, toys, books, electronics

Parking: Dedicated lot

Easy Access: Highway 50 to Mather Field Drive exit

Prices:

Comments: Traditional thrift store.

SACRAMENTO

THE THRIFT STORE #1
6606 Fruitridge Road
Sacramento, CA 95820
916-383- 3651

Web Address: None

Hours: Monday- Friday   9 - 9
                Saturday   10 - 6
                Sunday   11 - 6

Type of Store: Thrift, for-profit

Selection: Family clothing, furniture, housewares and accessories

Parking: Shared lot

Easy Access: Highway 50 to 65th Street exit South

Prices:

Comments: Lots of seasonal clothing at great prices.

Upscale   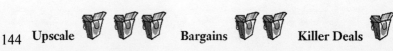 **Bargains**   **Killer Deals**

SACRAMENTO

THIS 'N THAT THRIFT AND GIFT
2590 21st Street
Sacramento, CA 95818
916-457-1877

Web Address: www.wix.com/tntthrift/tntwebpage

Hours: Tuesday - Saturday   10 - 6
                Sunday   12 - 4

Type of Store: Thrift, non-profit

Selection: Family clothing, shoes and accessories; jewelry, furniture, housewares, greeting cards, crafts books, linens, small appliances, records, eveningwear, some bridal

Parking: On street and rear parking lot

Easy Access: On 21st near X Street and Highway 50

Prices:

Comments: If you like incense, you will enjoy shopping here. Good selection of eveningwear and larger sizes.

Upscale **Bargains** **Killer Deals** 145

SACRAMENTO

THRIFT CENTER
2507 Del Paso Boulevard
Sacramento, CA 95815
916-920-0374

Web Address: None

Hours: Monday- Saturday   9 - 8
             Sunday   10 - 6

Type of Store: Thrift, for-profit

Selection: Family clothing, furniture, housewares, electronics, toys

Parking: Small strip center

Easy Access: Off El Camino at Highway 80

Prices: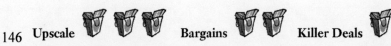

Comments: Lots of bargains for the family.

SACRAMENTO

THRIFT TOWN THRIFT STORE
410 El Camino Avenue
Sacramento, CA 95815
916-922-9942

Web Address: www.thrifttown.com

Hours: Monday- Friday   9 - 8
                Saturday   10 - 7
                Sunday   10 - 6

Type of Store: Thrift, for-profit

Selection: Large array of family clothing and shoes, accessories, small appliances, housewares, jewelry, sporting goods, books and records, collectibles; limited furniture

Parking: Large lot shared by King's Supermarket

Easy Access: On corner of Fair Oaks Boulevard/Marconi

Prices:

Comments: With over 4,000 recycled items arriving daily, there lots of shopping choices. Billed as "your first-class secondhand store", it's an updated thrift store presentation. Two other locations; Sacramento and Carmichael.

SACRAMENTO

THRIFT TOWN THRIFT STORE
5005 Stockton Boulevard
Sacramento, CA 95820
916-454-0435

Web Address: www.thrifttown.com

Hours: Monday- Friday   9 - 8
            Saturday   10 - 7
            Sunday   10 - 6

Type of Store: Thrift, for-profit

Selection: Large array of family clothing and shoes, accessories
small appliances, housewares, jewelry, sporting goods, books and
records, collectibles; limited furniture

Parking: Strip center

Easy Access: Just North of Fruitridge Road

Prices:

Comments: With over 4,000 recycled items arriving daily, there lots
of shopping choices. Billed as "your first-class secondhand store", it's
an updated thrift store presentation. Two other locations: Sacramento
and Carmichael.

 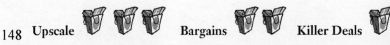

SACRAMENTO

THUNDERHORSE VINTAGE
2522 J Street
Sacramento, CA 95816
916-444-7723

Web Address: www.yelp.com/liz/thunderhorse-vintage- sacramento

Hours: Daily 12 - 7

Type of Store: Resale: buy, sell, trade

Selection: Strictly vintage items: clothing, toys, shoes, eyewear, accessories

Parking: On street

Easy Access: Mid-town Sacramento

Prices:

Comments: Hellbent for vintage for radical ladies and gnarly men, they say. If you are a Retro Rat, you'll love this store.

Upscale Bargains   Killer Deals 149

SACRAMENTO

VINTAGE YSJ
924 12th Street
Sacramento, CA 95814
916-442-4882

Web Address: www.vintageysj.com

Hours: Monday- Friday   11 - 6
                 Saturday   12 - 6
                 Sunday   Closed

Type of Store: Resale: buy, sell or trade

Selection: Women's vintage and contemporary clothing, shoes and accessories; some menswear

Parking: On street and in back alley

Easy Access: Midtown at 12th and J Streets

Prices:

Comments: A balance of old and new, young and hip, fashion-forward and retro in an historic Masonic Temple building.

 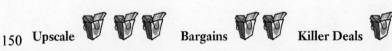

SACRAMENTO

WEAVE THRIFT
2401 Arden Way
Sacramento, CA 95825
916-643-4606

Web Address: www.weaveinc.org

Hours: Monday- Saturday   10 - 6
          Sunday   12 - 5

Type of Store: Thrift, non-profit

Selection: Family clothing, shoes and accessories; jewelry, housewares and home goods

Parking: Small strip mall

Easy Access: Between Fulton & Bell

Prices:

Comments: Updated thrift store.

SHINGLE SPRINGS

JENNI LYNN BOUTIQUE
4131 South Shingle Road
Shingle Springs, CA 95682
916-672-2844

<u>Web Address</u>: www.jennilynn.biz

<u>Hours</u>:

Monday- Friday	10 - 6
Saturday	10 - 5
Sunday	Closed

<u>Type of Store</u>: Consignment

<u>Selection</u>: Women's and juniors clothing, shoes, jewelry and accessories; prom dresses

<u>Parking</u>: Shingle Springs Shopping Center

<u>Easy Access</u>: Highway 50 to Shingle Springs exit

<u>Prices</u>: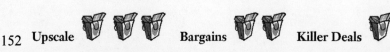

<u>Comments</u>: Lots of labels for the fashion-conscious.

SUTTER CREEK

INTERFAITH GRAPE VINES THRIFT
460 Highway 49
Sutter Creek, CA 95685
209-267-5970

Web Address: www.interfaithfoodbank.org

Hours: Monday- Friday   10 - 5
            Saturday   10 - 4
            Sunday   Closed

Type of Store: Thrift, non-profit

Selection: Family clothing, shoes and accessories; toys, books, housewares, linens, small appliances, furniture

Parking: Strip center

Easy Access: On Highway 49 at Sutter Hill next to Amador Athletic Club

Prices:

Comments: Traditional thrift store that used to be Trinity Treasures.

Upscale  Bargains Killer Deals

VACAVILLE

CONSIGNZ
372 Merchant Street
Vacaville, CA 95687
707-455-0500

Web Address: www.consignz.com

Hours: Tuesday - Saturday   10 - 5
            Sunday   Closed

Type of Store: Consignment

Selection: Women's clothing, shoes, accessories, jewelry; bed linens, furniture and home goods

Parking: Strip center

Easy Access: Off Highway 80 at Alamo Drive to Merchant Street

Prices:

Comments: Upscale boutique presentation at thrift store prices. A $3 rack in front draws you in, along with an unusually generous consignment split. Lots of labels and deals for frugal fashion femmes.

 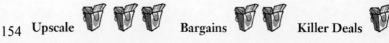

VACAVILLE

GOODWILL
1317 E. Monte Vista Avenue
Vacaville, CA 95688
707-455-0685

Web Address: www.goodwillsacto.org

Hours: Monday- Saturday   9 - 9
                Sunday   11 - 7

Type of Store: Thrift, non-profit

Selection: Large selection in every category - family clothing, shoes, and accessories; jewelry, electronics, housewares, small appliances, furniture, books toys, sporting goods

Parking: Large lot

Easy Access: Three blocks off Highway 80 at East Monte Vista Avenue

Prices:

Comments: Very traditional thrift store presentation in cheerful yellow/blue building. The number of labels will surprise you: Escada, Jones New York, Liz Claiborne, Chico. Prices are higher than Goodwill stores in Sacramento County.

Upscale   **Bargains**   **Killer Deals**   155

VACAVILLE

NORTH BAY GUILD THRIFT SHOP
409 Main Street
Vacaville, CA 95688
530-451-0462

Web Address: www.northbay.org

Hours: Tuesday - Friday   10 - 3
                    Saturday   9 – 3

Type of Store: Thrift, non-profit

Selection: Family clothing, shoes, accessories, housewares, jewelry

Parking: Lot next to the store

Easy Access: On Main Street in downtown Vacaville

Prices: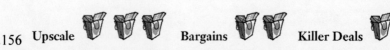

Comments: Traditional thrift store. Can't miss the bright blue exterior awning.

VACAVILLE

ONCE UPON A CHILD
2041-B Harbison Drive
Vacaville, CA 95687
707-448-1212

Web Address: www.onceuponachild.com

Hours:

Monday- Friday	9:30 - 7
Saturday	9:30 - 6
Sunday	11:00 - 5

Type of Store: Resale: buy and sell

Selection: Kids' clothing for newborns to sizes 16/18, shoes, accessories, equipment, books, toys

Parking: Large strip center

Easy Access: Off Highway 80 at Allison Drive next to Ross

Prices:

Comment: A one-stop shop for your little ones.

VACAVILLE

ST. PAUL'S THRIFT SHOP
120 West Street
Vacaville, CA 95688
707-448-3244

Web Address: None

Hours: Wednesday 12 - 4

Type of Store: Thrift, non-profit

Selection: Family clothing, shoes and accessories, books, housewares

Parking: Dedicated lot

Easy Access: Two blocks from downtown Vacaville

Prices:

Comments: Limited shopping on only one day in tiny two-story house. You can get an entire bag of goodies for only $5.

WEST SACRAMENTO

GOODWILL
3065 West Capitol Avenue
West Sacramento, CA 95691
916-374-0697

Web Address: www.goodwillsacto.com

Hours: Monday- Saturday   10 - 8
           Sunday   11 - 6

Type of Store: Thrift, non-profit

Selection: Family clothing, shoes, accessories, jewelry, furniture, electronics, toys, small appliances, housewares

Parking: Shared lot

Easy Access: Highway 50 to Harbor to West Capitol Avenue

Prices:

Comments: Traditional thrift store - great for bargain hunters.

CONSIGNMENT AND THRIFT STORES
CALIFORNIA: LAKE TAHOE AREA

SOUTH LAKE TAHOE

BARGAINS GALORE
972 Tallac Avenue
South Lake Tahoe, CA 96150
530-541-0444

Web Address: None

Hours: Monday- Saturday   10 - 4
                Sunday, Wednesday   Closed

Type of Store: Thrift, for-profit

Selection: Housewares, art, patio accessories, men's and women's clothing

Parking: Shared lot

Easy Access: Off South Lake Tahoe Boulevard

Prices:

Comments: Aptly named, "bargain" is also a verb; prices are negotiable.

SOUTH LAKE TAHOE

CONNIE'S CLOTHESLINE THRIFT STORE
854 Emerald Bay Road, #A
South Lake Tahoe, CA 96150
530-542-3030

Web Address: None

Hours: Monday- Friday   11 - 5
                Saturday   10 - 4
                Sunday   Closed

Type of Store: Thrift, for-profit

Selection: Select array of family clothing, home accessories, tapes/
cds, jewelry, sporting goods, seasonal clothing

Parking: Small strip center

Easy Access: On Highway 89 (Emerald Bay Road)

Prices:

Comments: Charming retail presentation at thrift prices.

SOUTH LAKE TAHOE

HOPE'S CLOSET AND THRIFT
2277 Lake Tahoe Boulevard
South Lake Tahoe, CA 96150
530-541-8937

Web Address: www.tahoeyouth.org

Hours: Tuesday - Saturday   10 - 5
             Sunday - Monday   Closed

Type of Store: Thrift, non-profit

Selection: Everything and anything: like-new family clothing from
infant to adults, formal and business wear, accessories, jewelry, home
furnishings

Parking: In front

Easy Access: Between Tahoe Keys Boulevard and Sierra
Boulevard

Prices:

Comments: Charming log cabin set in pine trees. Designed like a
boutique, priced like a thrift. Cozy bargain shopping.

KINGS BEACH

TAHOE FOREST HOSPITAL THRIFT
8611 North Lake Boulevard
Kings Beach, CA 96143
530-546-5494

Web Address: www.tahoeforesthospital.com

Hours: Monday- Saturday   10 - 5
             Sunday   10 - 4

Type of Store: Thrift, non-profit

Selection: Family clothing accessories and shoes; toys, books, electronics, small appliances, sporting goods, furniture

Parking: Dedicated lot

Easy Access: Across from the beach at Coon Street

Prices:

Comments: Traditional thrift store.

Upscale   Bargains   Killer Deals   163

TRUCKEE

MOUNTAIN KIDS
10095 Dorchester Drive
Truckee, CA 96161
530-550-7475

Web Address: www.mtnkidsonline.com

Hours: Tuesday - Saturday 10 - 6
             Sunday - Monday   Closed

Type of Store: Consignment

Selection: Children's clothing from newborns to teens, shoes and accessories, toys, books, equipment; women's clothing to size 16, shoes and accessories

Parking: Lot shared by Glenshire Store

Easy Access: Highway 80 to Central Truckee exit to Donner Pass Road to Glenshire

Prices:

Comments: Upstairs loft chock full of kids' stuff including earth-friendly items. Check out weekly story times. Another store in downtown Truckee.

TRUCKEE

MOUNTAIN KIDS/ECHO BLUE
11429 Donner Pass Road, #6
Truckee, CA 96161
530-550-5295

Web Address: www.mtnkidsonline.com

Hours: Tuesday - Sunday   10 - 6
           Monday   Closed

Type of Store: Consignment

Selection: Kids' clothing from infants to teens, shoes, accessories, toys, books, equipment, furniture, snow gear; women's maternity and regular clothing, shoes, accessories and jewelry

Parking: On street and in shared lot

Easy Access: Highway 80 to Donner Pass Road

Prices:

Comments: Two stores in one: kids' boutique and edgy women's junior fashions in Echo Blue. Lots of handmade accessories and new kids' birthday gifts.

TRUCKEE

TAHOE FOREST HOSPITAL THRIFT
10026 Meadow Way
Truckee, CA 96161
530-582-4947

Web Address: www.tahoeforesthospital.com

Hours: Monday- Saturday   10 - 5
                Sunday   10 - 4

Type of Store: Thrift, non-profit

Selection: Family clothing, shoes and accessories; skiwear, toys, electronics, small appliances, sporting goods, furniture

Parking: Dedicated lot

Easy Access: Off Donner Pass Road

Prices:

Comments: Traditional thrift store with upscale brands and large selection of skiwear.

Upscale   **Bargains**   **Killer Deals**

TRUCKEE

THRILL OF THE FIND THRIFT
11429 Donner Pass Road, #3
Truckee, CA 96161
530-587-3145

Web Address: None

Hours: Monday-Saturday   10 - 5
                Sunday   11 - 4

Type of Store: Resale: buy and sell

Selection: Family clothing, shoes and accessories; housewares, sporting goods, toys, electronics, furniture, some designer skiwear

Parking: Strip mall, West Gate Center

Easy Access: Off Highway 80 at Donner Pass exit

Prices:

Comments: Upscale clothing including skiwear for the entire family.

Upscale   Bargains   Killer Deals   167

TRUCKEE

UNIQUE BOUTIQUE/VIVIANE'S VINTAGE &VOGUE
10925 West River Street
Truckee, CA 96161
530-582-8484

Web Address: None

Hours: Tuesday - Saturday   11:30 - 6
                Sunday - Monday   Closed

Type of Store: Consignment

Selection: Women's vintage and contemporary clothing to size 2X, shoes and accessories; jewelry, costumes, lingerie; some menswear

Parking: Large lot

Easy Access: Highway 89 to West River Street, follow pink finger signs pointing the way

Prices:

Comments: Known as "theme party central" by regular customers since 1984, this is fun shopping with a view of the river.

CONSIGNMENT AND THRIFT STORES
NEVADA: LAKE TAHOE AREA

INCLINE VILLAGE

PRESBYTERIAN WOMEN'S THRIFT SHOP
799 Southwood Boulevard
Incline Village, NV 89451
775-831-3902

Web Address: None

Hours: Monday- Saturday   11 - 3
                Sunday   Closed

Type of Store: Thrift, non-profit

Selection: Family clothing, shoes and accessories; housewares, toys, books, electronics, sporting goods, some furniture

Parking: In strip mall

Easy Access: Off Tahoe Boulevard in Village Shopping Center close to Post Office

Prices:

Comments: Traditional thrift store; cast-offs from upscale Incline Villagers.

INCLINE VILLAGE

TAHOE FAMILY SOLUTIONS
797 Southwood Boulevard
Incline Village, NV 89451
775-833-4414

Web Address: None

Hours: Monday- Saturday   11 - 4
                Sunday   Closed

Type of Store: Thrift, non-profit

Selection: Family clothing, shoes and accessories; toys, books,
jewelry, electronics, small appliances, sporting goods

Parking: Dedicated lot

Easy Access: Off Tahoe Boulevard

Prices:

Comments: Traditional thrift store.

 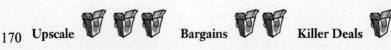

CONSIGNMENT AND THRIFT STORES
NORTHERN NEVADA

CARSON CITY

CLASSY SECONDS THRIFT SHOP
41 Hot Springs Road
Carson City, NV 89706
775-841-7081

Web Address: www.classyseconds.com

Hours: Monday- Friday   9 - 5
                  Saturday   9 - 4
                  Sunday   10 – 3

Type of Store: Thrift, non-profit

Selection: Family clothing, shoes and accessories, housewares, small appliances, toys, sporting goods, jewelry

Parking: Small strip mall

Easy Access: Off Highway 395 South

Prices:

Comments: Traditional thrift store.

 Upscale   Bargains   Killer Deals

CARSON CITY

DAISY'S THRIFT STORE
1991 Highway 50 East, #2
Carson City, NV 89701
775-883-2520

Web Address: None

Hours: Monday- Saturday 9 - 5
        Sunday   Closed

Type of Store: Resale: buy and sell

Selection: Family clothing, shoes and accessories; furniture, housewares, electronics, toys, books, small appliances, sporting goods, tools, movies

Parking: Large lot

Easy Access: On Highway 50 East between Rand and Humboldt Lane near AT & T

Prices:

Comments: Traditional thrift store presentation; prices are negotiable.

 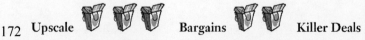

CARSON CITY

FISH THRIFT STORE
138 East Long Street
Carson City, NV 98701
775-882-3474

Web Address: www.nvfish.com

Hours: Monday- Saturday   9 - 5
        Sunday   Closed

Type of Store: Thrift, non-profit

Selection: Family clothing, shoes and accessories; jewelry, toys, books, housewares, electronics, furniture, sporting goods

Parking: Dedicated lot

Easy Access: On East Long Street at Carson Street

Prices:

Comments: Traditional thrift store; also in Gardnerville and Mound House.

Upscale   Bargains   Killer Deals   173

CARSON CITY

THE IVY COVERED COTTAGE SENIOR THRIFT
911 Beverly Drive
Carson City, NV 89706
775-882-0151

Web Address: None

Hours: Monday- Saturday   10 - 3:30
                Sunday   Closed

Type of Store: Thrift, non-profit

Selection: Family clothing, furniture and accessories

Parking: Large lot next to Senior Center

Easy Access: Off Long and East Roop

Prices:

Comments: Very traditional thrift store.

CARSON CITY

ORMSBY ASSOCIATION THRIFT STORE
930 East Corbett Street
Carson City, NV 89706
775-882-6955

Web Address: www.ormsbyarc.org

Hours: Monday- Friday   10 - 3
             Saturday   10 - 4
             Sunday   Closed

Type of Store: Thrift, non-profit

Selection: Family clothing, shoes and accessories; electronics small appliances, sporting goods, furniture, linens, books, toys, tools

Parking: In front

Easy Access: At Roop and Corbett Streets

Prices:

Comments: Traditional thrift store in distinctive blue building.

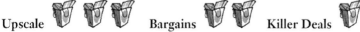

CARSON CITY

SALVATION ARMY
190 Winnie Lane
Carson City, NV 89706
775-885-1898

Web Address: www.salvationarmy.com

Hours: Monday- Saturday   10 - 6
                Sunday   Closed

Type of Store: Thrift, non-profit

Selection: Family clothing, shoes and accessories; furniture, small appliances, sporting goods, linens, books, toys, tools, electronics, housewares

Parking: Dedicated lot

Easy Access: Off Highway 395 South behind Safeway

Prices:

Comments: Traditional thrift store.

 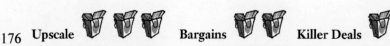

FALLON

FALLON INDUSTRIES THRIFT STORE
165 South Main Street
Fallon, NV 89406
775-423-8211

Web Address: www.fallon industries.org

Hours: Monday- Friday   9 - 5
            Saturday   9 - 4
            Sunday   Closed

Type of Store: Thrift, non-profit

Selection: Family clothing, shoes and accessories; toys, housewares, books, electronics, small appliances, sporting goods

Parking: Dedicated lot

Easy Access: On Main Street at Williams Street

Prices:

Comments: Located in an historic building; second location in Fernley.

Upscale Bargains Killer Deals

FERNLEY

FERNLEY INDUSTRIES THRIFT STORE
1301 Financial Way
Fernley, NV 89408
775-575-7000

Web Address: www.fallonindustries.com

Hours: Monday- Friday   9 - 5
             Saturday   9 - 4
             Sunday   Closed

Type of Store: Thrift, non-profit

Selection: Family clothing, shoes and accessories; toys, books, electronics, small appliances, furniture, sporting goods, housewares

Parking: On street and in back of store

Easy Access: Highway 50 to Farm District Road

Prices:

Comments: Follow the huge "Thrift Store" sign. Sister store in Fallon.

 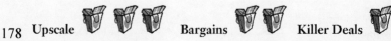

FERNLEY

JERRY'S BARGAIN BIN AND THRIFT

878 Highway 95 North, #A
Fernley, NV 89408
775-575-4499

Web Address: None

Hours: Monday- Saturday   9 - 5
                Sunday   Closed

Type of Store: Thrift, non-profit

Selection: Family clothing, accessories and shoes; electronics, housewares, books, toys, small appliances, sporting goods, furniture, linens, tools

Parking: In front in small strip center

Easy Access: Highway 95 North to Cottonwood

Prices:

Comments: Looks are deceiving - small from the outside but a ton of treasures on the inside.

GARDNERVILLE

HELPING HANDS THRIFT SHOP
1418 Industrial Way, #A
Gardnerville, NV 89410
775-782-9410

Web Address: None

Hours: Monday- Saturday   10 - 5
              Sunday   Closed

Type of Store: Thrift, non-profit

Selection: Family clothing, shoes and accessories; housewares, small appliances, toys, books, sporting goods

Parking: On street

Easy Access: Industrial Way at Meeks on Highway 395 South

Prices:

Comments: Traditional thrift store.

 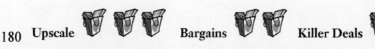

GARDNERVILLE

FISH THRIFT STORE
1231 Service Drive
Gardnerville, NV 89410
775-783-1455

Web Address: www.nvfish.com

Hours: Monday- Saturday 9 - 6
        Sunday   1 - 4

Type of Store: Thrift, non-profit

Selection: Family clothing, shoes and accessories; housewares, furniture, electronics, small appliances, toys, books, sporting goods

Parking: Dedicated parking lot

Easy Access: Off Highway 395 South at Service Drive

Prices: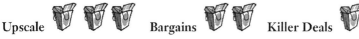

Comments: Traditional thrift store with other locations in Carson City and Mound House.

Upscale Bargains Killer Deals   181

MINDEN

FLIP FLOP THRIFT AND EXCHANGE
1609 Highway 395 North, #B
Minden, NV 89423
775-392-0371

Web Address: www.flipflopthrift.com

Hours: Monday- Friday   9:30 - 4
              Saturday   9:30 - 2
              Sunday   Closed

Type of Store: Thrift, for profit

Selection: Family clothing, shoes and accessories; housewares, small appliances, sporting goods, furniture, linens, books, toys, tools, electronics

Parking: Shared lot

Easy Access: Highway 395 North past Carson Valley to Buckeye

Prices: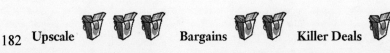

Comments: Updated thrift presentation.

MOUND HOUSE

FISH THRIFT STORE
10126 Highway 50 East
Mound House, NV 89403
775-246-7654

Web Address: www.nvfish.com

Hours: Monday- Saturday   9 - 5
               Sunday   Closed

Type of Store: Thrift, non-profit

Selection: Family clothing, accessories and shoes; furniture, jewelry, toys, books, electronics, housewares

Parking: Dedicated lot

Easy Access: Near Blue Mountain steel factory

Prices:

Comments: Updated traditional thrift store with lots of antiques, collectibles, jewelry and better womenswear; also in Carson City and Gardnerville.

RENO

ASSISTANCE LEAGUE THRIFT SHOP
1701 Vassar Street
Reno, NV 89502
775-329-6658

Web Address: www.assistanceleaguerenosparks.org

Hours: Monday- Saturday   10 - 4
        Sunday   Closed

Type of Store: Thrift, non-profit

Selection: Family clothing, shoes and accessories; housewares, small appliances, books, toys, furniture

Parking: Dedicated lot

Easy Access: On Vassar Street at Harvard across from Channel 4 TV station

Prices: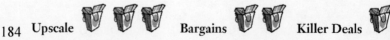

Comments: Known as "the Nordstrom of local thrift stores" among thrift shoppers.

RENO

CLOTHES MENTOR
1509 South Virginia Street
Reno, NV 89502
775-284-0680

Web Address: www.clothesmentor.com

Hours: Monday- Saturday   10 - 7
         Sunday   11 - 6

Type of Store: Resale: buy and sell

Selection: Women's clothing and accessories

Parking: Larger center shared by Sports West

Easy Access: On South Virginia Street and Mt. Rose Street

Prices:

Comments: Upscale womenswear in boutique setting, sizes
0 - 3X. Located next door to Plato's Closet (same owner).

RENO

ENCORE BOUTIQUE
267 Vassar Street
Reno, NV 89502
775-284-9454

<u>Web Address</u>: None

<u>Hours</u>:   Tuesday - Saturday   10 - 5
                 Sunday - Monday   Closed

<u>Type of Store</u>: Consignment

<u>Selection</u>: Women's clothing, shoes and accessories; jewelry, some housewares

<u>Parking</u>: On street

<u>Easy Access</u>: On Vassar Street between Holcomb and South Wells Avenue

<u>Prices</u>: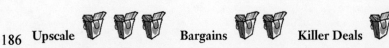

<u>Comments</u>: Charming intimate shopping with a room devoted to plus sizes.

RENO

GOODWILL
6407 South Virginia Street
Reno, NV 89551
775-853-7606

Web Address: www.goodwill@gimi.org

Hours: Monday- Saturday   9 - 8
          Sunday   11 - 6

Type of Store: Thrift, non-profit

Selection: Family clothing, shoes and accessories; toys, furniture, small appliances, electronics, sporting goods, housewares

Parking: Large strip mall across from Whole Foods

Easy Access: On South Virginia at Neil Road

Prices:

Comments: Updated traditional thrift store - great for bargain hunters.

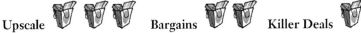

Upscale   Bargains   Killer Deals

RENO

JUNKEE CLOTHING EXCHANGE
9605 South Virginia Street
Reno, NV 89502
775-322-5865

Web Address: www.junkeeclothingexchange.com

Hours: Daily 11 - 7

Type of Store: Resale: buy, sell, trade

Selection: Men's and women's clothing, shoes and accessories; jewelry, costumes

Parking: On street and dedicated lot

Easy Access: On South Virginia Street near Holcomb in former Reno Restaurant Supply building

Prices:

Comments: 8,800 square feet of recycled shopping in a hip, eclectic setting (3,000 square feet of which is an antiques and collectibles co-op). Energetic and highly creative displays.

 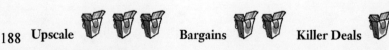

RENO

LABELS CONSIGNMENT BOUTIQUE
601 West 1ˢᵗ Street
Reno, NV 89501
775-825-6000

Web Address: www.labelsreno.com

Hours: Monday- Friday   10 - 6
            Saturday   10 - 5
            Sunday   11 - 4

Type of Store: Consignment

Selection: Upscale women's clothing, shoes and accessories; jewelry, eveningwear

Parking: On street and dedicated lot

Easy Access: Across from Truckee River downtown Reno

Prices:

Comments: Reno's oldest and finest upscale consignment store is a fashionista's dream. More designer labels than a metro store three times its size.

RENO

ONCE UPON A CHILD
6015 South Virginia Street, #G
Reno, NV 89502
775-825-4448

Web Address: www.onceuponachild.com

Hours: Monday- Saturday   9:30 - 7
            Sunday   11:00 - 5

Type of Store: Resale: buy and sell

Selection: Kids' clothing, shoes and accessories; furniture, toys, equipment

Parking: Large lot in Del Monte Plaza

Easy Access: On South Virginia Street near Whole Foods

Prices:

Comments: Everything for kids from newborns to sizes 16/18 youth. A one-stop shop for your little ones.

RENO

PLATO'S CLOSET
1535 South Virginia Street
Reno, NV 89509
775-322-0110

Web Address: www.platosclosetreno.com

Hours: Monday- Saturday   10 - 9
               Sunday   11 - 9

Type of Store: Resale: buy, sell, trade

Selection: Young men's and women's clothing, shoes and accessories

Parking: Large strip center shared by Sports West

Easy Access: On South Virginia Street at Mt. Rose Street

Prices:

Comments: Junior focus with lots of small sizes for slender shoppinistas. Located next to Clothes Mentor (same owner).

RENO

RIDGE HOUSE THRIFT STORE
900 West 1st Street
Reno, NV 89503
775-322-8941

<u>Web Address</u>: www.ridgehouse.org

<u>Hours</u>:	Monday- Friday	9 - 5
	Saturday	10 - 7
	Sunday	12 - 5

<u>Type of Store</u>: Thrift, non-profit

<u>Selection</u>: Family clothing, shoes and accessories; furniture, books, toys, small appliances, linens, tools, housewares

<u>Parking</u>: On street and in back

<u>Easy Access</u>: Off Keystone Avenue

<u>Prices</u>:

<u>Comments</u>: Traditional thrift store.

 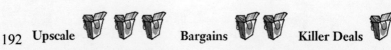

RENO

SAVERS
3800-200 Kietzke Lane
Reno, NV 89502
775-284-4350

Web Address: www.savers.com

Hours: Monday- Saturday   9 - 9
              Sunday   10 - 7

Type of Store: Thrift, for profit

Selection: Family clothing, shoes and accessories; furniture, books, housewares, small appliances, toys, linens

Parking: Large strip center

Easy Access: On corner of Kietzke Lane/East Peckham Lane

Prices: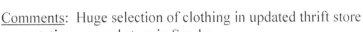

Comments: Huge selection of clothing in updated thrift store presentation; second store in Sparks.

Upscale   Bargains 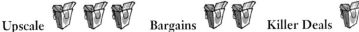 Killer Deals   193

RENO

SPCA OF NORTHERN NEVADA THRIFT STORE
401 Vine Street
Reno, NV 89503
775-324-7776

<u>Web Address</u>: spcanevada.org

<u>Hours</u>:

Monday- Saturday	9 - 4:45
Sunday	Closed

<u>Type of Store</u>: Thrift, non-profit

<u>Selection</u>: Family clothing, shoes and accessories; books, toys, furniture, electronics, housewares, sporting goods, pet accessories

<u>Parking</u>: Large strip center

<u>Easy Access</u>: On the corner of West 4th and Vine Streets at Sportsman's Corner

<u>Prices</u>:

<u>Comments</u>: Traditional thrift store.

RENO

ST. VINCENT'S THRIFT SHOP
500 East 4th Street
Reno, NV 89512
775-322-9824

Web Address: www.catholiccharitiesnorthernnevada.org

Hours: Monday- Saturday   8:30 - 4:50
            Sunday   Closed

Type of Store: Thrift, non-profit

Selection: Family clothing, shoes and accessories; small appliances, housewares, books, toys, furniture, electronics, tools

Parking: Dedicated lot

Easy Access: Corner of Valley Drive and East 4th Street

Prices:

Comments: Traditional thrift store.

Upscale   Bargains   Killer Deals   195

RENO

THE THRIFT DEPOT
575 East 4th Street
Reno, NV 89512
775-786-4499

Web Address: None

Hours: Monday- Saturday   9:30 - 6:30
                Sunday   Closed

Type of Store: Thrift, non-profit

Selection: Family clothing, shoes and accessories; books, toys, furniture, small appliances, electronics, linens, housewares

Parking: On street or in adjacent lot

Easy Access: East 4th Street at Elko Street, four blocks east of Silver Legacy Hotel Casino

Prices:

Comments: Very large traditional thrift store in distinctive white/ green building. Also stores in Sparks and Sun Valley.

RENO

W.A.R.C.THRIFT STORE
560 Gentry Way
Reno, NV 89502
775-825-1972

Web Address: www.highsierraindustries.com

Hours: Monday- Saturday   9:30 - 6:30
            Sunday   11:00 - 6:00

Type of Store: Thrift, non-profit

Selection: Family clothing, accessories and shoes; furniture, electronics, housewares small appliances, sporting goods, linens, books, toys, tools

Parking: Shared parking lot in strip center

Easy Access: On Gentry Lane at Kietzke Lane

Prices:

Comments: Traditional thrift store. With three locations in Reno.

RENO

W.A.R.C. THRIFT STORE
201 Keystone Avenue
Reno, NV 89503
775-358-9050

Web Address: www.highsierraindustries.com

Hours: Monday- Saturday   9:30 - 6:30
                Sunday   10:00 - 6:00

Type of Store: Thrift, non-profit

Selection: Family clothing, shoes and accessories; toys, books, kitchenware, furniture, small appliances, linens, books, electronics, small appliances

Parking: On street

Easy Access: At Keystone Avenue and West 2nd Street 2 blocks from Truckee River

Prices: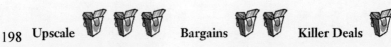

Comments: Traditional thrift store. With three locations in Reno.

Upscale  **Bargains** **Killer Deals**

RENO

W.A.R.C. THRIFT STORE
790 Sutro Street
Reno, NV 89512
75-333-8262

Web Address: www.highsierraindustries.com

Hours: Monday- Saturday   9:30 - 6:30
                Sunday   11:00 - 6:00

Type of Store: Thrift, non-profit

Selection: Family clothing, shoes, accessories; housewares, electronics, sporting goods, small appliances

Parking: Lot adjacent to store

Easy Access: East 9th Street to Sutro Street near Highway 80 overpass at Wells Avenue

Prices:

Comments: Traditional thrift store. With three locations in Reno.

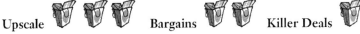
Upscale   Bargains   Killer Deals   199

SPARKS

EASTER SEALS THRIFT
2150 Oddie Boulevard
Sparks, NV 89436
775-825-7774

Web Address: www.sierra.eastseals.com

Hours: Monday- Saturday   9:00 - 7:30
              Sunday   10:00 - 5:00

Type of Store: Thrift, non-profit

Selection: Family clothing, shoes and accessories; jewelry, housewares, electronics, small appliances, toys, books, sporting goods, furniture

Parking: Large strip mall

Easy Access: Oddie Boulevard at Sullivan

Prices:

Comments: Traditional thrift store with an expanded selection of furniture.

SPARKS

GOODWILL
2424 Oddie Boulevard, #C
Sparks, NV 89512
775-358-6444

Web Address: www.gimi.org

Hours: Monday- Saturday   9 - 8
             Sunday   11 - 6

Type of Store: Thrift, non-profit

Selection: Family clothing, shoes and accessories; furniture, electronics, toys, books, small appliances, sporting goods, housewares

Parking: Plentiful in large strip center

Easy Access: On Oddie Boulevard at Silverada Boulevard close to Highway 395 North

Prices:

Comments: Very traditional thrift store.

 Upscale   Bargains   Killer Deals

SPARKS

SAVERS
2359 Oddie Boulevard
Sparks, NV 89431
775-359-4244

Web Address: www.savers.com

Hours: Monday- Saturday   9 - 9
                    Sunday   10 - 7

Type of Store: Thrift, for-profit

Selection: Family clothing, shoes and accessories; furniture, toys, books, small appliances, housewares, linens

Parking: Large lot in Silverada Mall

Easy Access: On Oddie Boulevard at El Rancho near Lowe's

Prices:

Comments: Huge selection of clothing in an updated thrift store presentation; second location in Reno.

SPARKS

THE THRIFT DEPOT
640 Greenbrae Drive
Sparks, NV 89431
775-331-5020

Web Address: None

Hours:
	Monday- Saturday	9:30 - 6:30
	Sunday	Closed

Type of Store: Thrift, non-profit

Selection: Family clothing, accessories, shoes; books, toys, sporting goods, electronics, small appliances, tools, housewares

Parking: Large lot

Easy Access: Greenbrae Drive at Pyramid next to Sparks Justice Court

Prices:

Comments: Traditional thrift store. Also stores in Reno and Sun Valley.

SUN VALLEY

THE THRIFT DEPOT
5105 Sun Valley Boulevard
Sun Valley, NV 89433
775-674-6444

Web Address: None

Hours: Monday- Saturday   9:30 - 6:30
                Sunday   Closed

Type of Store: Thrift, non-profit

Selection: Family clothing, shoes and accessories; books, toys, small appliances, furniture, housewares

Parking: Large lot

Easy Access: On Sun Valley Boulevard at 2nd Street in Dollar Loan Center

Prices:

Comments: Traditional thrift store. Also stores in Reno and Sparks.

Jo Anna Philips, a popular author and speaker, is a former newspaper columnist, feature writer, TV and radio host. She was a retail buyer for a major fashion chain prior to designing and manufacturing her own line of women's sportswear, Giovanna Activewear, in San Francisco.

Other books by **Jo Anna Philips**:

How to Shop for the Perfect Relationship:
The Ultimate Dating Guide for Men and Women

Available on www.amazon.com and www.joannaphilips.com

CPSIA information can be obtained at www.ICGtesting.com
Printed in the USA
269333BV00001B/32/P